GOOD · OLD · DAYS®

# Live It Again™

# 1954

# Dear Friends,

Life was first-rate in what many folks warmly recall as the "nifty '50s," and this was especially true in 1954, a pivotal year. Folks were optimistic about the future. Many were blessed with fat paychecks, had extra money in their pockets, and were in the mood to spend it. Americans were encouraged to buy not just to meet basic needs, but also to make their dreams come true. Consumer culture was in full bloom as we bought, bought, bought!

In 1954, some 1.5 million homes were built. Contractor Bill Levitt supercharged the construction industry with his brainchild, the suburb. Many left the city for a new home in the suburban oasis of middle-class families. A suburban house was a bargain, and the community was roomy enough for every child to experience the great outdoors. The winding streets were lined with neat little one-family houses on small squares of green grass.

*Consumer culture was in full bloom as we bought, bought, bought!*

The number of homes with television soared to 29 million, double the number in use three years before. Along with the surge in television viewing came a new way of cooking: the TV dinner. Those little aluminum trays of frozen food were a mom's secret weapon for coping with busy days. There was no prep time. She just pulled them from the freezer and popped them into the oven. In the evenings, families often crowded around the flickering light of the black-and-white TV to watch their favorite shows and eat steaming-hot TV dinners.

The Chevrolet Corvette sprang onto the scene. It was the first all-American sports car and became a legend in the automobile industry. The two-seater with a fiberglass body was gorgeous and on the wish lists of many, along with the other car models shown on pages 22 through 27.

Memories take us back to a world gone away. We've packed this edition of *Live It Again* with wonderfully nostalgic images that will unleash a flood of memories from the thriving days of 1954. Take pleasure in the flashback to an exciting year when life was good, and the living was easy.

# Contents

6 1954's Top Tunes

8 The Television Craze

14 On the Radio

16 Technology

20 Cover Artist, Thornton Utz

22 The Rubber Meets the Road

28 Urban Life

30 Home Havens

34 Modern conveniences

36 What Made Us Laugh

38 Mr. President, Dwight D. Eisenhower

40 On the Job

44 Romance

48 Our Faith

50 Family Life

56 1954 Shopping Experience

58 Convenience Foods

60 Rural Living

62 Fun Festivities

66 Vacation Memories

REPRINTED WITH PERMISSION OF ALLIS-CHALMERS ENERGY IN

**68** Americans Travel

**72** What Made Us Laugh

**74** In the News

**80** Bob Hope, Thanks for the Memories

**82** The Big Screen

**84** Unforgettable Icons

**90** The Best in Sports

**94** What Made Us Laugh

**96** Leading Ladies of *The Post*

**98** Fashionable in 1954

**104** When I Grow Up …

**106** School Days

**110** The Clubs We Joined

**112** Leisure Activities

**114** Child's Play

**118** Yuletide Memories

**120** More *The Saturday Evening Post* Covers

**124** More Famous Birthdays

**126** Facts and Figures of 1954

REPRINTED WITH PERMISSION FROM FORD MOTOR COMPANY

# 1954 Quiz

1. What show was on both TV and radio during 1954?

2. Which all-American sports car had a fiberglass reinforced body?

3. What was the top movie at the box office in 1954?

4. Who played Jeff Miller in the TV show Lassie?

5. What company had luxury buses called Scenicruisers?

6. What was the top TV show in 1954?

7. "Mambo Italiano" was made famous by what singer?

8. What famous actress got married on Sept. 25, 1954?

*Answers appear on page 127*

© 1954 SEPS

REPRINTED WITH PERMISSION OF FEDERAL-MOGUL CORPORATION

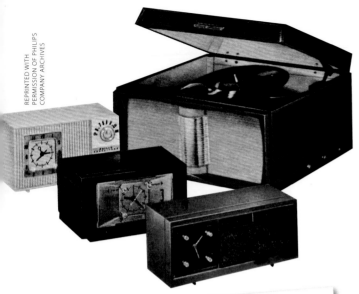

# 1954's Top Tunes

A variety of music filled the homes and hearts of Americans in 1954, with more than 20 million families buying half-a-billion records during the year. Bill Haley & His Comets found fame with the song "Shake, Rattle and Roll," the top hit of the year. Entertainment was synonymous with Frank Sinatra. His song "Young at Heart" was such a hit that a movie was renamed to the song title. The Crew-Cuts recorded "Sh-boom," and their version of the song topped the Billboard charts for nine weeks during August and September. The Chordettes, an all-girl singing group, rocketed to major chart success with "Mr. Sandman."

The Crew-Cuts sang in barbershop-quartet style. The group's name came from their identical haircuts.

## Top Hits of 1954

**"Shake Rattle and Roll"**
Bill Haley & His Comets

**"Young at Heart"**
Frank Sinatra

**"Sh-Boom"**
The Crew-Cuts

**"Goodnight, Sweetheart, Goodnight"**
The Spaniels

**"Mr. Sandman"**
The Chordettes

**"Mambo Italiano"**
Rosemary Clooney

**"Stranger in Paradise"**
Tony Martin

**"Three Coins in the Fountain"**
The Four Aces

**"Oh, My Papa"**
Eddie Fisher

**"Naughty Lady of Shady Lane"**
The Ames Brothers

1954 Trivia

**Q.** Who wrote the "Shake Rattle and Roll" lyrics?

A. Big Joe Turner

Joey Ambrose, Johnny Grande, Billy Williamson, Bill Haley, Marshall Lytle and Dick Richards. Bill Haley was the least likely of the early rockers to succeed in that genre. A former yodeler and small-town disc jockey, he sported a spit curl that looped over his forehead.

The Chordettes began their career on *Arthur Godfrey's Talent Scouts* TV show in 1949, sticking to traditional a cappella barbershop repertoire.

Cool and collected, Frank Sinatra worked hard to maintain the standards he set with sold-out concerts.

Groucho Marx quizzed contestants on *You Bet Your Life*. He often described his once-a-week appearance on television as "a soft racket."

## 1954 Trivia

**Q.** How many seasons was *I Love Lucy* the No. 1 TV show?

A. Four seasons—
1952, 1953, 1954 and 1956

Lucille Ball and Desi Arnaz are shown during a 1954 performance of *I Love Lucy*. During the 1954 TV season, Ricky Ricardo, played by Desi Arnaz, was scripted to become more successful. Desi received a movie offer that prompted a cross-country trip by car with his TV wife, Lucy, played by his real-life wife, Lucille Ball.

TV entertainer Jackie Gleason, left, performs on his own show. His variety hour was recorded live in New York and aired on TV on Saturdays at 8 p.m. His often-used catchphrase was, "How sweet it is!"

# The Television Craze

Television was in the midst of its "Golden Age" in 1954 with a mixture of comedy, drama and variety shows. *I Love Lucy* was the top-rated television show, as it was in four of its six seasons. It was the first scripted TV show shot in front of a live studio audience, and it aired on Monday nights at 9. Lucille Ball played her role of a wacky housewife who made life difficult for her loving, but perpetually irritated husband, Ricky Ricardo, played by her real-life husband Desi Arnaz. "Away we go!" was both trademark and battle cry of top-rated comic Jackie Gleason. Taking off each week with elbows akimbo, Gleason reigned as "Mr. Saturday Night." Comedian Groucho Marx was the emcee and star of the quiz show, *You Bet Your Life*, seen on Thursday nights at 8. The series' most important asset was the humor injected by Groucho into the interviews he did with contestants before they played the game.

## Tops on Television

*I Love Lucy*
**CBS**

*The Jackie Gleason Show*
**CBS**

*Dragnet*
**NBC**

*You Bet Your Life*
**NBC**

*The Toast of the Town*
**CBS**

*Disneyland*
**ABC**

*The Jack Benny Show*
**CBS**

*The George Gobel Show*
**NBC**

*Ford Theatre*
**NBC**

*December Bride*
**CBS**

Actresses Frances Rafferty, left, and Spring Byington read through a stack of cookbooks during an episode of *December Bride*. It was a show about an attractive widow, played by Byington, and her social life.

## Television Shows Debuting in 1954

*Annie Oakley*

*The Brighter Day*

*The Public Defender*

*Justice*

*The Mickey Rooney Show*

*It's a Great Life*

*Willy*

*Lassie*

*The Tonight Show*

*The Imogene Coca Show*

*The Jimmy Durante Show*

*Flash Gordon*

*Father Knows Best*

*The Adventures of Rin Tin Tin*

*Climax!*

*Disneyland*

*Face the Nation*

*The Secret Storm*

# The Television Craze

## Debuts

A large number of television shows debuted in 1954. Favorite long-running children's adventure series, *Lassie*, was introduced and revolved around a brave, loyal and remarkably intelligent collie named Lassie. *Father Knows Best* was a wholesome, family situation comedy featuring the Andersons, an idealized family that viewers could relate to and emulate. The basic setting of *The Jimmy Durante Show* was a small nightclub. In the role of club operator, Jimmy interviewed and auditioned talent. Steve Allen was the original host of *The Tonight Show*. Under Allen, the show was very informal and aired Monday through Friday at 11:30 p.m. He would open each evening seated at the piano, chatting and playing some of his own compositions.

*Lassie* was the story of a young boy and his companion collie. The boy was Jeff Miller, played by Tommy Rettig, who lived on a small farm with his widowed mother, played by Jan Clayton, and grandfather, played by George Cleveland.

© GETTY IMAGES

Jimmy Durante, in the photo at left, is surrounded by showgirls. His raspy voice and large "schnozzola," or nose, were his trademarks.

© GETTY IMAGES

Brook Byron, as Althea Dennis, acted in *The Brighter Day*, a TV soap opera seen on weekday afternoons. Involving a lengthy list of characters, the show emphasized the Dennis Family.

© GETTY IMAGES

GETTY IMAGES

The cast of *Father Knows Best*, clockwise from lower left: Billy Gray as James "Bud" Anderson Jr., Elinor Donahue as Betty "Princess" Anderson, Robert Young as Jim Anderson, Jane Wyatt as Margaret Anderson and Lauren Chapin as Kathy "Kitten" Anderson. The show was on Sundays at 10 p.m.

Comedian and talk show host Steve Allen is seated at a desk during an episode of *The Tonight Show*. The emphasis was on Steve and his comedic ad-libbing.

This Stromberg-Carlson television, priced from $249.95, featured panoramic vision for room-wide viewing.

# SYLVANIA Makes the Only Television Sets that Give Your Eyes the Comfort of "SURROUND LIGHTING"

This Exclusive Use of SURROUND LIGHTING is Called

## HaloLight

HaloLight is a translucent frame around the TV screen that is softly illuminated from the back by a specially designed fluorescent light.

HaloLight makes the picture look larger and clearer. It reduces the sharp contrast between the bright screen and the surrounding darkness. The result is wonderfully restful and pleasing to your eyes.

A great step forward in viewing comfort — and only Sylvania TV has it. Another Sylvania first!

The STRATFORD – Beautiful 21" Natural Blonde Korina Console with HaloLight. Also in Mahogany. Sylvania Television sets are priced as low as $179.95. Slightly higher West and South.

# SYLVANIA TELEVISION

HaloLight is a Sylvania Trademark

Sylvania Electric Products Inc., 254 Rano Street, Buffalo 7, New York • RADIO • TELEVISION • LIGHTING • ELECTRONICS

HENRY BOLTNOFF

"Alfred's hobby is fixing things beyond repair!"

Exclusive Bendix "HI-DIAL" ALL CONTROLS ABOVE THE SCREEN

A Bendix television picked up reception in areas where the nearest station was far away. The model also had controls above the screen and sold for $179.95.

# The Television Craze

## The new models

The number of homes with television increased to 29 million, double the number in service three years before. No other household technology had ever spread so rapidly into so many homes. Commercial color television became a reality with the first coast-to-coast color-cast from the Pasadena Tournament of Roses Parade in California on New Year's Day. The market for color sets was still small, though, due to the average selling price of $900. Viewers seeing color shows in black-and-white were aware of such advantages as a greater sense of depth and a sharper picture. Better picture quality and engineering evolved into television viewing that was easy on the eyes.

Light and compact, this Emerson TV was priced at $129.

Zenith televisions were known for having one standard of quality, regardless of price.

COURTESY OF ZENITH

The Capehart television, made by International Telephone and Telegraph Corp., combined radio, phonograph and television into a stylish piece of furniture with doors that closed. It sold for $895.

RCA's three-way television combined TV, radio and phonograph for $399.50.

# On the Radio

In order to compete with television, new trends in programming marked the year in radio. "Across the board," or five-a-week schedules, began for *Fibber McGee and Molly*, *Amos 'n' Andy* and other shows. Fans of the radio show *Dragnet* remember the memorable and distinguished voice cadence of police Sgt. Joe Friday. The series covered crimes from petty theft to murder and used the most complex sound effects in the industry. Mike Wallace, known for his role on the television show *60 Minutes*, began his radio career by announcing serialized radio dramas. Alan Freed was the energetic DJ who coined the phrase "rock and roll" in the 1950s, and not only sparked the musical trend, but fanned it into flame.

Disc jockey Alan Freed's late-night show on WINS in New York was called the *Rock 'n' Roll Party*.

American broadcast journalist Mike Wallace speaks into a microphone for the radio program *On a Sunday Afternoon*.

## The Metro Daily News

FINAL EDITION

JANUARY 14, 1954

### NEW YORK YANKEE JOE DIMAGGIO MARRIES ACTRESS MARILYN MONROE.

The marriage ended in divorce before the close of 1954.

# Radio Stars & Hits of 1954

*Amos 'n' Andy*

Bing Crosby

*Dragnet*

Edgar Bergen and Charlie McCarthy

*Escape*

*Falcon*

*Fibber McGee and Molly*

*Gunsmoke*

*The Lone Ranger*

*Mr. Keen, Tracer of Lost Persons*

*The Shadow*

*Sherlock Holmes*

*Suspense*

*The Whistler*

*Yours Truly, Johnny Dollar*

© GETTY IMAGES

Jack Webb was the star of *Dragnet*, which was a hit radio and television show simultaneously in 1954. The program was one of the first law-enforcement dramas in entertainment. It brought police danger and heroics into the homes of Americans, influencing popular opinion of police departments across the country.

Zenith offered small radios with quality sound that sold for as little as $19.95. Portable radios kept listeners up-to-date on news and the latest tunes.

## "Is it for ME?"

You kind of hope it is—for good news and good times often come your way by telephone.

Maybe it's a date for sister Sue. Or a business call for Dad. Or Bill asking if Jimmie can go to the movies. Or Grandma calling Mother to find out if things are all right. And everything is more likely to be all right when there's a telephone in the home.

In many, many ways, the telephone is a real friend of the family. And the cost is small—just pennies a call.

**BELL TELEPHONE SYSTEM**
LOCAL *to serve the community.* NATIONWIDE *to serve the nation.*

FAMOUS BIRTHDAYS
Christie Brinkley, February 2
model and actress
John Travolta, February 18 actor

A call flashes on the switchboard, and the operator connects to the correct party.

Telephone booths were available for phone calls for those who could not afford their own phone or needed to make a call when out of town. Charges ranged from a nickel to a dime.

# Technology

## Everyone's talking on the horn

In 1954, manual exchange subscribers placed calls through an operator, who connected the parties using a switchboard. Operators would say, "Number please." In an emergency, the operator would have the number traced and the street address confirmed. Then she plugged in a special trunk to the police. Emergencies were handled by operators night and day. A party line was an arrangement in which two or more customers were connected directly to the same local loop. Those with party telephone lines learned the fascination of listening in on their neighbors. They also learned to converse guardedly, on the assumption their neighbors were eavesdropping.

Long-distance rates for three minutes after 6 pm and all day Sunday ranged from 40 cents for a New York to Philadelphia call to $2 for San Francisco to Washington, D.C.

Send your voice where your thoughts are

It was good to share in all the news as if you were there in person.

"Oh, we're through talking. We're just listening to see who hangs up first."

# Technology

## Cameras for everyone

A teenager records a family reunion with a camera.

In 1954, the camera became one of the most common props of civilization. In this country, the camera business achieved an annual-dollar pinnacle of about a half billion for amateur demands alone. Approximately two of every three families in the United States owned one or more cameras. Photos were predominately black-and-white, but because of color's relatively fast rise, the proportion in color was at an all-time high. Teenagers shot flash pictures of each other all the time, including at the milk bar and at basketball games. They even packed the cameras to dances. Of course, they couldn't afford fine cameras, but they certainly gave their box cameras a workout, burned bulbs and had fun.

A new Argus projector with the carrying case sold for $66.50. It showed, changed and stored color slides automatically.

Americans shot about two billion pictures in 1954. This Argus 35mm camera was perfect for color slides, black-and-white pictures and action shots, and it was priced at $66.50.

1954 ARGUS INC.

**The Metro Daily News**

THE WEATHER

FINAL EDITION

FEBRUARY 17, 1954

CIGARETTE MANUFACTURERS ANNOUNCE THE FORMATION OF THE TOBACCO INDUSTRY RESEARCH COMMITTEE.

This committee was formed in response to a rash of reports blaming smoking for lung cancer.

The new, low-cost, pocket-size, picture-in-a-minute Polaroid camera sold for about $70.

Some people set up improvised darkrooms in their homes to develop their photos.

The Anscoflex modern reflex camera featured double-exposure prevention and sold for about $15.

The busiest photographer in the country was the American housewife. She took her black-and-white film to the drugstore or mailed it to Sears for developing.

# Cover Artist, Thornton Utz

Thornton Utz was born in the southern town of Memphis, Tenn. At age 12, Thornton created a comic strip that he distributed to neighborhood kids. He graduated from high school in 1933 and later attended the American Academy of Art in Chicago. Young Utz worked his way into a steady position in advertising by moving from one print shop to the next. Signing an agent in 1944, he received his first big magazine assignment by illustrating a short story for *The Saturday Evening Post*. Utz's first *Post* cover was for the Sept. 10, 1949, edition and is shown on the upper left side of page 20. The 1950s brought prosperity to the country as a whole, and Thornton's knack for capturing the humorous in everyday situations fueled his personal success. During this period he produced 45 covers for *The Post*.

# The Rubber Meets the Road

The common-sense Willys station wagon could be used for family transportation or as a work car, with ample space for tools or bulky packages.

A DeSoto took you from dead stop to highway-speed fast, without the slightest lag or hesitation, for about $2,923.

The new Nash Rambler "Cross Country" was spacious with a travel rack for extra luggage.

For the last ten years the problem had been to produce enough cars to supply the demand in the face of war, shortages and high public buying power. In 1954, the race to supply the demand was finally won. The problem was now to sell the huge number of autos coming off assembly lines. But automotive leaders continued to be confident of their industry's future. They pointed out that while suburban living had made two cars a necessity for many families, only 12 percent of current owners had two cars.

COURTESY OF CHRYSLER GROUP LLC

COURTESY OF CHRYSLER GROUP LLC

COURTESY OF CHRYSLER GROUP LLC

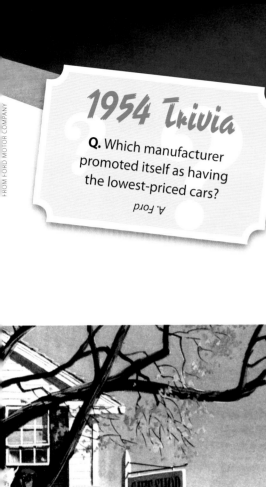

Ford cars featured styling for which you'd expect to pay hundreds more, such as soundproofed interiors, and durable upholsteries and trim. Base price was $2,165.

*Dollar for Dollar*

*You Can't Beat a*

# PONTIAC

The Pontiac Chieftain station wagon was big, smart and superlatively well-built.

# The Rubber Meets the Road

## *Sports cars*

COURTESY OF CHRYSLER GROUP LLC

REPRINTED WITH PERMISSION FROM GENERAL MOTORS COMPANY

Oldsmobile's Super "88" was long and low-level. Spirits went up when convertible tops went down.

Exuberant new color and bold sweep of line drew the eye like a magnet to this Chrysler convertible.

**FAMOUS BIRTHDAYS**
**Catherine Bach, March 1** actress (Daisy Duke of *Dukes of Hazzard*)
**Ron Howard, March 1** actor, director and producer (Opie of *The Andy Griffith Show* and Richie of *Happy Days*)

REPRINTED WITH PERMISSION OF STUDEBAKER NATIONAL MUSEUM

Studebaker's low-swung styling won outstanding awards in international competitions including both American and foreign cars.

REPRINTED WITH PERMISSION FROM FORD MOTOR COMPANY

Mercury's Sun Valley, America's first transparent-top car, sold for a base price of $2,582.

The Pontiac Star Chief convertible was an all-out favorite of roving, sun-loving Americans from coast to coast.

The 1954 Buick Skylark convertible had advanced styling with power steering and brakes, along with power operation of windows and top. It sold for $4,483.

The Chevrolet Corvette, above, was the first all-American sports car with a fiberglass reinforced body. Base price for the Corvette was $2,774. The Chevrolet Bel Air Convertible, left, packed high-compression power under the hood.

# The Rubber Meets the Road
## Classy automobiles

There were numerous options for those who could afford any car and wanted performance, luxury and lasting qualities. Owning such a car was a symbol of wealth immediately recognized by all who saw it. Multitudes dreamed of owning such a car. Pictured at right is the stunning New Yorker DeLuxe Newport by Chrysler.

COURTESY OF CHRYSLER GROUP LLC

The 1954 Buick Roadmaster was an impressive automobile in size, length, breadth and beauty.

REPRINTED WITH PERMISSION FROM GENERAL MOTORS COMPANY

The 1954 Kaiser was advertised as "the new car with the big change!" Those modifications included a more powerful motor, new French-style headlights and the largest glass area of any standard American sedan.

What made a 1954 Cadillac stand out from other cars? It was a 50-year policy of adherence to the highest ideals in engineering, manufacturing and service. The base price of a Cadillac Eldorado was $5,738.

The Packard, below, was priced from $3,230 to $3,400.

**The Metro Daily News**

THE WEATHER
City will be unsettled. Snow. Cold.
Much in front diverse

VOLUME 57 — No. 161

FINAL EDITION

16 PAGES          FIVE CENTS

MARCH 13, 1954

## MILAN HIGH SCHOOL WINS THE INDIANA STATE BASKETBALL TITLE.

Milan High School (enrollment 161) defeats Muncie Central High School (enrollment over 1,600) 32-30. The 1986 movie *Hoosiers* was loosely based on this Milan team.

A single city building, at right, housed numerous floors filled with a variety of businesses. Bustling Houston, below, was the only United States city of more than 250,000 people with no zoning laws in 1954.

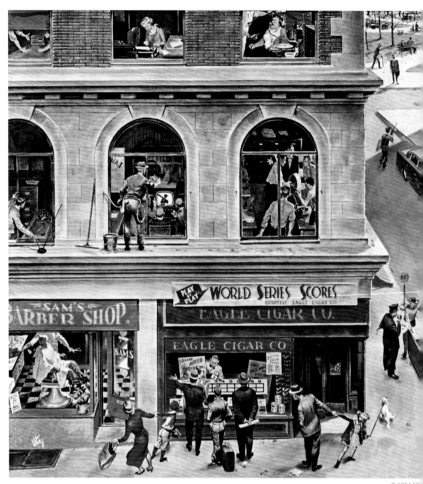

© 1954 SEPS

© 1954 SE

Street scene shown in Manhattan's traffic-choked garment district. New York suburbs were growing fast in 1954, but the city wasn't being deserted. It was simply overflowing.

# Urban Life

Cities displayed soaring art-deco skyscrapers and the glass-and-steel towers that rose up after the war. Tall buildings, along with rail stations, hotel lobbies and sidewalks were standard in most cities. Along with access to theaters, clubs and department stores, many city dwellers coped with traffic issues. Many traveled by bus and were happy to let bus drivers negotiate the streets. Some cities were well-known for their travel challenges. The motorists of Los Angeles could do 55 mph through the center of town on a $3 million-a-mile freeway system. How they loved the "Stack," a revolutionary new traffic intersection, where 32 lanes of traffic went in eight directions at once.

## 1954 Trivia

**Q.** What large city was reported to have the worst traffic tangle in 1954?

A. Los Angeles

An evening on the town often included dining at a fine restaurant and attending an opera.

# Home Havens

## Suburban living

The postwar suburbs were, in many ways, a frontier. The people who moved there forged a new way of life in a new landscape. Most of the families thought of themselves as middle class. Everyone lived on the same side of the tracks, and there were no slums to fret about or families of conspicuous wealth to envy. Levittown, Pa., was the best-known large suburb. In the neighborhoods they designed, Levitt & Sons incorporated curvilinear roads that did not have four-way intersections. There were a total of about 16,000 homes, 12 schools, eight churches and five big swimming pools.

Bill Levitt, above, was often credited as the creator of the modern American suburb. What set his second project, Levittown, Pa., apart from other developments at the time was that it was built as a complete community.

In 1954, most heads of household in the Levittown suburb were under 30 and the majority of youngsters were not yet 5 years old.

"You'll find this a very friendly neighborhood."

A typical suburban home was one level, with a street-side picture window and an attached garage.

## The Metro Daily News

**FINAL EDITION**

### APRIL 12, 1954

# BILL HALEY & HIS COMETS RECORD "ROCK AROUND THE CLOCK"

This well-known classic is known as the anthem for rebellious 1950s youth.

# Home Havens

## Interior design

Parents were being crowded out of their living rooms by the growing size and activity of American families. To give them a hideout all their own, the upstairs parlor was born. Lighting became more modern with wall sconces, drop lights from the ceiling, cornice lights over the window draperies and recessed ceiling spotlights. Bathrooms grew in size. The deluxe version pictured on the facing page included a concealed automatic washer and dryer to let you keep up with your laundry where it collected. Popular home flooring options included floor tiles that were easily cleaned, durable and could be homeowner-installed for about $16.75 for an 8 x 10-foot room. Various synthetic fibers were also used in the new carpet textures, though cotton and wool remained popular. Linoleum was another type of floor covering that was widely used.

"This is interesting. This article says that 63% of all accidents occur in the home."

With families growing larger in number and spending more time at home, Americans began to want a house as big as the outdoors. Nature's own color scheme brought the outdoors into the home.

# Home Havens

## Modern conveniences

1954 was in the midst of a decade of one of history's greatest shopping sprees. Many Americans adorned their mass-produced homes with all sorts of modern conveniences. There were so many things to buy—a power lawn mower, a stove with a double oven, a dishwasher or a vacuum cleaner. Products were available in a rainbow of colors and a steadily changing array of styles. A happy homeowner was one with a house filled with labor-saving appliances and a thriving family.

The Rheem Coppermatic water heater supplied a nearly continuous flow of hot water.

Whether renting, remodeling or building, there was a KitchenAid dishwasher to fit any kitchen.

**FAMOUS BIRTHDAYS**
**Jackie Chan, April 7** martial arts expert and actor
**Vince Ferragamo, April 24** NFL quarterback

About 1.4 million power lawn mowers were sold in 1954. The models below ranged in price from $104.50 to $227.50.

The latest Frigidaire electric range offered easy, accurate top-of-range cooking along with two-oven convenience. Color choices were white, yellow or green.

The big rubber wheels of the Lewyt vacuum cleaner took the hard work out of vacuuming. It swiveled and rolled easily from room to room without catching, tipping or scratching.

# What Made Us Laugh

"Now that you're earning more, dear,
I feel we can finally afford to be in debt."

"One hundred and fifty cups of flour, fifty cups
of milk, two hundred and fifty egg whites,
five hundred and ten tablespoons of shortening …"

"How's that for power?"

"She'll be down in a few minutes …
although, frankly, I can't see why!"

"Good thing we got popcorn—that'd be mighty sickening on an empty stomach!"

"George is very fastidious."

"Afraid some of my grass cuttings blew over into your yard, Miss Henshaw."

"You could leave it like this and call it the 'Rainbow Room'!"

President Eisenhower celebrated his 64th birthday on Oct. 14, 1954.

President Eisenhower signs H.R. 9757, an amendment to the Atomic Energy Act of 1946. The signing was witnessed in his office by various senators, congressmen and members of the Atomic Energy Commission.

John Foster Dulles, Prime Minister Winston Churchill, President Eisenhower and Anthony Eden enjoy the outdoors while discussing world peace at the White House in June.

President Eisenhower pauses for the camera as he works on a painting of his daughter-in-law Barbara and grandchildren David, Anne and Susan.

# Mr. President, Dwight D. Eisenhower

After two years serving as president, Ike learned that persuasion and compromise were not enough, that even a president had to be a politician. In June of 1954, President Eisenhower and Prime Minister Churchill conferred at Washington, D.C., on world peace. In an effort to eradicate the American Communist Party, President Eisenhower signed the Communist Control Act. Oct. 25th was the first telecast of a cabinet meeting. With the assistance of Congress, the president also sought to transform the atom from a scourge into a benefit for mankind with his Atoms for Peace program. The purpose was to widen cooperation with allies in atomic energy matters and improve procedures for control of atomic energy information.

President Eisenhower and his wife, Mamie, at the White House on May 27, 1954.

The President usually held press conferences, attended by nearly 200 reporters, on Wednesdays. If he was not prepared to answer a question, he would explain why.

# On the Job

## His scene

The average income of men, which had been rising steadily since the end of World War II, leveled off in 1954 at $3,967. Housing construction and the network of jobs related to that field soared as families grew. Another large area of jobs existed in the auto industry with major car companies experiencing huge volumes of orders. Men sought employment with the frame of mind that if they worked hard, earned a good salary with employer-paid benefits and adhered to "company policy," they would be ensured a job for a lifetime.

This equipment operator's job is to dig a cellar for a new house, but the work is halted by pleading for the salvation of the local sandlot.

Some men who lived along the seashore fished for a living. Others manned lighthouses to provide light as an aid in navigation of the sea or inland waterways.

The Metro Daily News

FINAL EDITION

THE WEATHER
City and State—Warm.
Some Cooler

VOLUME 41 — No. 166

FIVE CENTS

MAY 24, 1954

IBM UNVEILS ITS VACUUM-TUBE ELECTRONIC "BRAIN," CAPABLE OF PERFORMING 10,000 FUNCTIONS PER HOUR

The fire department's annual dance is interrupted by an emergency. Though the job can be dangerous, the men will likely return as heroes to again embrace their dear ones at the dance.

Electric-company workers kept vital electricity flowing to the increasing number of homes and businesses.

As airline travel was becoming more common, the number of planes and pilots increased.

"Home Beauty Jamborees," head-to-toe beauty demonstrations, were staged in local communities. Women of all ages were shown how to bring out their "hidden beauty."

Secretaries knew shorthand and used the method to record employers' letters and instructions that were later typed.

"Boy, when this one said 'Personal,' it meant Personal."

REPRINTED WITH PERMISSION FROM INTERNATIONAL PAPER

# On the Job

## Her scene

More women were entering the workforce as businesses thrived and grew. Jobs in retail sales, customer service, bookkeeping and office administration, purchasing, secretarial and accounting were part of the necessary operation of most businesses. Other women joined the ranks of air stewardesses, nurses and teachers. Among women, the median income in 1954 was estimated at $1,200. Since the close of World War II, the average income of women increased by about $250, or 30 percent.

Women who craved adventure became stewardesses. They could travel and meet all sorts of people.

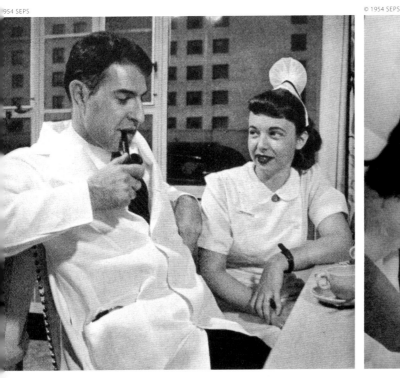

There was a shortage of nurses in 1954, even though nursing offered security and generally good working conditions.

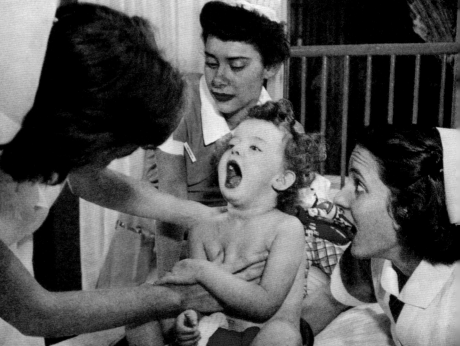

A cooperative young patient submits cheerfully to a thorough check-up for nursing students.

Dating is exciting and adventurous when a motorcycle and a beach are combined.

# Romance

## The courtship

When a boy found one girl more interesting and enjoyable than others, dating became important. Most couples began by going on a double date with another couple, which made it easier to think of interesting things to say and do. Initially, there was a lot of laughter and talk, and the conversation seldom turned serious. Regular pair dating was the next step, when a couple wanted a chance to get to know each other in more depth. Dating became an important part of preparation for marriage. It provided an opportunity to learn about the moods, plans and dreams of the opposite sex. Knowledge gained from dates helped with making a wise choice when selecting a partner for life.

Conversations via telephone often led to a date. Couples sometimes dressed formally when going out, and it was proper etiquette for boys to open doors for girls.

Bicycles built for two were a romantic choice for a summer date.

**FAMOUS BIRTHDAYS**
Jeff Apple, May 10 producer
Jackie Slater, May 27 NFL offensive tackle

For couples who enjoyed the outdoors, picnics in the shade were a good activity choice.

County fairs were popular summer dating spots, especially when a couple could sit close on the Ferris wheel.

Pretty young bride Mary Freeman, champion swimmer, and groom, Olympic medalist and brother of Grace Kelly, John B. Kelly Jr., cut their ornate, tiered wedding cake. The average age for first marriages was 23 for men and 20 for women.

Actress Audrey Hepburn wed actor-filmmaker Mel Ferrer on Sept. 25, 1954. Twenty-five guests were invited to join the couple for their wedding ceremony and reception in Switzerland.

The honeymoon will take place in a state of bliss despite the pranksters who tied tin cans behind the nuptial automobile. Yet how sweet is the tin-can music as the newlyweds drive to their destination.

John Clymer

The Metro Daily News
FINAL EDITION

JUNE 19, 1954

BETTY JAMESON, NATIVE OF NORMAN, OKLA., WINS LPGA WESTERN GOLF OPEN

# Romance

## The wedding day

Golden Globe- and Academy Award-winning actress Audrey Hepburn married Mel Ferrer in 1954. Her wedding dress, a gown featuring a tiny waist, puffed sleeves and full skirt, was a trendsetter. The dress was a sweet tea-length that matched her pixie-length hair decorated with fresh flowers. The shorter length was a great way to show off fun shoes. A popular honeymoon destination in 1954 was Niagara Falls. The location became an oasis for couples and was called the "Honeymoon Capital."

It's time for the honeymoon, and the eager groom stands by the door with the luggage, ready to be on his way.

"Oh, sorry … I guess I'm a little excited."

Family and friends give the bride and groom a proper send-off at the airport.

Sunday school attendance increased as more parents brought their children to church to learn more about God and faith.

# Our Faith

Acknowledgment of a Supreme Being became part of the Pledge of Allegiance in 1954 when President Eisenhower signed an act adding the words "under God." This addition portrayed a renewed interest in religious conviction. The United States was becoming a godlier nation, with an increase in church members. There was more awareness of God in both public and private sectors. Why was this happening? Some credited the increased use of TV and radio for religious messages. Maybe the best explanation was given by Methodist Church bishops who said, "A new spirit has fallen upon the people."

Deep in the heart of America there was an inspiring revival. The country church was coming back to life.

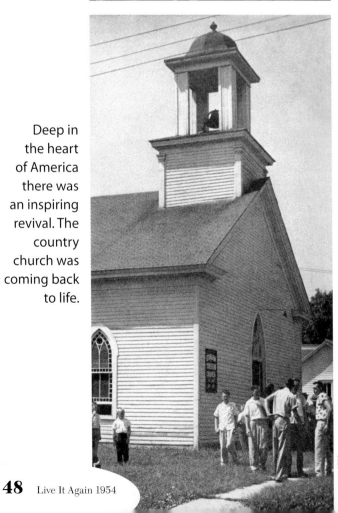

Children fold their hands and learn to pray as demonstrated by their mother.

PIN THE TAIL

# Family Life

There is rarely a dull moment in a home where children are present. Ideas for mischief are doubled and tripled when siblings collaborate. We sometimes invaded a sibling's bedroom to turn the furniture upside down or place a perfectly preserved dead snake near the bed and wait to hear the scream. Those times when we made strange noises outside a window just to watch the reaction of those inside were a hoot, especially when Dad would nick himself while shaving and Mom dropped shells in the scrambled eggs. Though rain during a birthday party panicked Mom, we thought the deluge made the celebration more fun.

Junior wakes his parents in a startling fashion with a toot of his trumpet. He thinks it's beneficial for them to be blasted out of bed 20 minutes early.

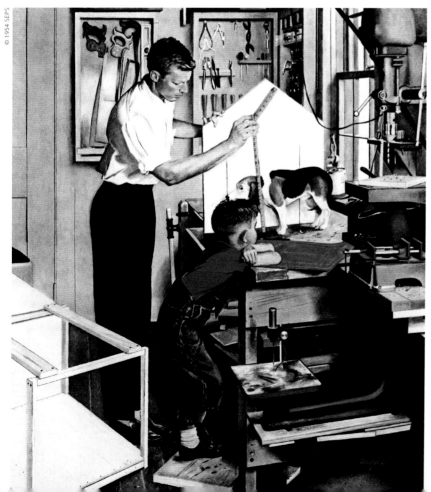

"Dependents … HALT!"

In this day of improved tools, the doghouse project gets quite complex and even includes blueprints.

# Family Life

## Fun moments

In 1954 the term "togetherness" gained some media legitimacy. It meant the family was a unit, and that Mom and Dad and the kids shared activities. Group activities helped create families that stayed together. Siblings were handy playmates and memories were sweeter when shared with others. Fun was as near as the backyard and swing set. It meant the world to a child to have Dad nearby when learning to ride a bike. Mom's smiles and applause while practicing a musical instrument encouraged budding musicians.

It is heartwarming to see how this boy trusts his father to halt that bicycle before both teacher and pupil land on their ears.

Giggles and the splash of cold water made bobbing for apples an invigorating fall event.

"I'm getting bored ... let's go over to your house!"

"Please, just push me one more time," the children beg, and devoted parents take time to comply.

Dad is a convenient "horse" for the tots to ride on while acting out their Wild-West adventures.

Father should be thankful. After all those music lessons, his offspring are forming a band. He just didn't anticipate that his once peaceful evenings would become quite so noisy.

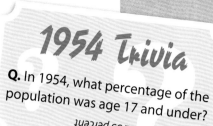

## 1954 Trivia

**Q.** In 1954, what percentage of the population was age 17 and under?

A. 33 percent

It may take the rest of the day for this mother to clean the kitchen, but the children and their friends are enjoying themselves so much, the task won't seem quite so tiresome.

# Family Life

## Mom's busy day

Her hands are busy at the stove, and her eyes are on the clock. Watch the toast. Time the eggs. Feed the children. Another day as a mother begins. TV personality Allen Ludden noted in one of his advice books that a teenage girl "knows that as a woman she will be doing a great deal more for others than will be done for herself." How true. In between keeping order in the home, she cans, cleans, sews for the family and washes an unending supply of dirty laundry. What would we do without her?

Three cheers for Mom, who has been busy all day canning produce for a winter of good eating.

This budding little genius dreams up a way to walk in the rain and still stay dry.

Women often sewed all of the family's clothes and altered them as the children grew.

Mom deserves a break during a busy day of homemaking.

"Can't hang them outside in this weather."

# 1954 Shopping Experience

For many Americans, a shopping trip was an expensive and time-consuming task when they lived far from stores. For them, the mail-order catalog was a blessing indeed. Anything needed could be ordered and delivered by mail right to the home. Items could also be ordered by phone, which produced faster service. At the large retail stores, merchandise was on display and ready for immediate selection and featured one-stop shopping. Small mom-and-pop stores were havens filled with treasures yet to be discovered. The variety of goods available in 1954 helped make shopping an enjoyable activity.

She is envisioning herself in the dress from the window display. He is picturing an evening alone with his sweetheart.

Mothers appreciate having groceries carried to the car, especially when supervising a number of children while shopping.

This catalog form was from a 1954 Montgomery Ward catalog. Items available through the catalog included clothes, furniture, appliances, toys, beauty supplies, bathroom fixtures, tools and even auto supplies.

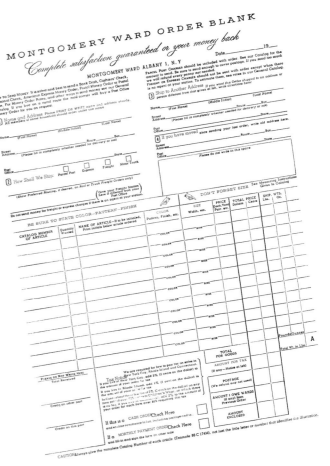

Women liked well-lit, convenient grocery stores that included background music to put them in a happy mood for shopping.

Air-conditioned comfort along with the convenience of such diversity under one roof lured customers to department stores.

Minute Rice was foolproof and required no washing, rinsing, draining or steaming. Homemakers could quickly bake a batch of chewy brownies when they bought Betty Crocker's mix. The ad above promoted the new product with an offer to buy one, get one at half price. Coffee was available in an instant. Just mix together a spoonful of granules and water for a quick hot beverage.

# Convenience Foods

Fixing food for the family became easier than ever in 1954. Women everywhere appreciated how convenience foods lightened their workload. Thanks to a unique type of aluminum packaging, housewives were able to prepare complete, piping-hot TV dinners for their families in minutes instead of hours. Betty Crocker's revolutionary new brownie mix was given rave reviews for being chewy and fudgy. Bakers who used the mix could get perfect brownies every time. Cooks could get homemade flavor and goodness with no mixing or extra dishes to wash, when they used refrigerated biscuits from a tube.

Mothers could serve home-baked biscuits in just 10 minutes to delight a hungry family.

Swanson TV Dinners were popular because they combined time-saving appliances and the public's interest in television. More than 10 million TV dinners were sold in 1954, the first year of national distribution for about $.98 each.

# Rural Living

The family farm was a busy place in spring, summer and fall as families planted, weeded and harvested crops. During the winter, the pace slowed somewhat. Another harvest was finished, and it was time to do chores that had been neglected, such as equipment repairs. Some families also milked cows, a seven-day-a-week job, to generate more revenue. To supplement the crop and critter income, families occasionally grew apples in country orchards. All hands were required to pick, sort and sell fruit. Bushels were set aside for making applesauce. Store-bought applesauce couldn't compete with the flavor of homemade applesauce.

"When that harvest sun's a-beating, thirsts are mighty hard to chase! What goes best with he-man eating? Seven-Up at every place!" read a 7UP advertisement.

An apple-eating country boy fishes in a creek near his home with his dog for company.

The Metro Daily News

FINAL EDITION

THE WEATHER

VOLUME 97 — No. 181

30 PAGES      FIVE CENTS

JULY 7, 1954

## ELVIS PRESLEY IS HEARD ON THE AIRWAVES FOR THE FIRST TIME

... when Memphis station WHBQ plays Elvis' first studio recording, "That's All Right (Mama)."

C·J·STERNB

A judge examines Hereford cattle, deciding which will receive the prized blue ribbon.

Children ride a pint-sized version of the Ferris wheel and can see the entire fair from a bird's-eye view.

Russell Pettit, manager of California's Santa Clara County Fair, and Bozo the Clown hobnob with Kids' Day customers.

**FAMOUS BIRTHDAYS**
**Walter Payton, July 25** NFL running back (Chicago Bears)
**Ken Olin, July 30** actor (Michael of *thirtysomething*)

# Fun Festivities

## Fairs and circuses

Summer seemed incomplete without a trip to the county fair. The delicious scents from concessionaires tempted visitors to sample corn dogs, elephant ears, cotton candy and popcorn. Barns were filled with cattle, hogs, bunnies and nanny goats, along with the proud 4-H kids who hoped to win ribbons by showing their animals. People strolled through the grounds to see the home-economics exhibits and new machinery. Another anticipated summer adventure was the traveling circus. All manner of exotic animals came to town along with their trainers, brightly dressed clowns and trapeze artists.

"The circus is in town!" shouted the townspeople as circus workers removed items from trucks and set up the tents.

Trainer George Keller works with the lions and tigers, a feature of the traveling circus.

# Fun Festivities

## Summer highlights

By midsummer, the sun's heat enveloped us. This was the weather for cooling drinks and barbecue served with the fresh taste of the outdoors. There was so much to do during the hot-weather months, and so little time to fit it all in. Swimming pools and beaches filled with folks looking for a way to cool down. People rode their bikes instead of driving cars, combining fresh air and exercise. A popular summer activity in 1954 was water skiing, and it made quite a splash in the vacation activities of more agile Americans. Don't forget summer camp. Remember staying in cabins, learning to swim and enjoying nature?

Summer camp was a time when youngsters could spread their wings a bit, though they likely missed Mom and Dad before the end of the week.

Mother and daughter visit the beach, and the baby's bottle needs warmed. The concession worker obliges, reluctantly.

"He buried a bone here last week."

Water skiing became popular. Some people owned their own equipment, while others rented a boat, skis and life jackets.

Summer fun at the beach is interrupted by a thunderstorm. Beachgoers pack up and run for shelter.

**The Metro Daily News**

FINAL EDITION

THE WEATHER
City and State—Hot,
Dusk, Cloudy
Details in Daily Almanac

VOLUME 87—No. 201

FIVE CENTS

AUGUST 16, 1954

## PUBLISHER HENRY LUCE LAUNCHES THE NATIONAL SPORTS MAGAZINE, *SPORTS ILLUSTRATED*

Families run to reach the last free table in the picnic area of the park. Is it worth it to battle for a spot among the multitude of people when the goal was to enjoy the the great outdoors and get away from it all?

© 1954 SEPS

© 1954 SEPS

Vacation was the perfect time to relax around a hotel swimming pool and watch the kids swim and dive. Watch out for splashes!

"I'm afraid we'll have to eat and run—I forgot my wallet."

FRANK
RIDGEWAY

© 1954 SEPS

# Vacation Memories

Summer included vacation time for many families. There was a certain charm in driving through mountains, valleys, farmland and cities to enjoy a week or so of new sights and experiences. Sometimes getting to the chosen vacation spot could be tedious. At right, Grandpa and Grandma are enjoying a leisurely drive in the country, while others are anxious to arrive at their destinations. Others chose to bypass the driving altogether, and opted for railroad or air travel. Some families vacationed by staying at motels and hotels, and dining in restaurants, while others beat the high cost of travel by camping out and cooking their own food.

Children are enjoying a camping vacation in the great outdoors. Parents might have had their hands full getting them all to go to sleep.

This is "wagons West" 1954 style. A trip with the whole family required efficient packing and lots of togetherness.

# Americans Travel

Due to the cost of airplane tickets, most Americans sought other ways to travel. Buses and trains were less expensive options, though more people chose bus travel. On a travel bus, patrons could look out the huge, tinted picture windows to view the road ahead or lean back and watch the passing scenery. Those who chose train travel could speed along without a worry. Some railroads offered a reduced ticket price for families. Two of the most popular destinations were San Francisco and Yosemite National Park.

Luxury buses called Scenicruisers, by Greyhound, went into service along thousands of miles of American highways. They were advertised as having living-room luxury with the glorious sensation of raised-level, panoramic sightseeing.

The Santa Fe Railroad offered smooth, swift, streamlined luxury travel. Every modern
travel convenience was available, including wonderful food and a nurse service.

Railroad bar cars offered live entertainment. These cars were
so popular that passengers slipped aboard early to get a seat.

People traveled by railroad in the easy-chair comfort of reclining
seats in Vista-Dome passenger cars that featured larger
windows for more expansive views of the passing landscape.

Economical and efficient grill cars were
replacing costly diners on some trains.

Ten times every day giant Pan American clippers spanned the Atlantic. Planes had luxurious lounges, and mothers appreciated the bassinets for babies.

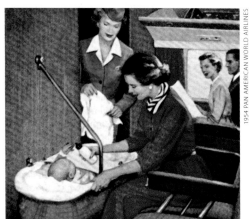

With that right-at-home feeling conveyed by United Air Lines through roomy and restful accommodations, you weren't just a passenger, but an honored guest.

"You'll travel the nation's largest, most completely modern commercial air fleet whenever you fly American Airlines," an ad announced.

# Americans Travel

## By plane

Prosperity gave Americans the means to enlarge their travel horizons. With generally only a couple of weeks of vacation at their disposal, they wanted to reach their destinations quickly, and that translated into air travel. Travel to foreign countries became more common. One-way fare from New York to Europe ranged in price from $290 to $360. Americans could fly away from winter to "sunshine lands" to visit such South American cities as San Juan, Rio de Janeiro and Buenos Aires. Due to the cost, air travel was affordable for only the most wealthy.

Mom and all the children traveled at half fare with TWA, which helped to make journeys by plane a family affair.

Travelers enjoyed red carpet service on United Air Lines' new DC-7s, the nation's fastest airliners in 1954. The planes cruised at 365 miles per hour. Luggage received "white glove treatment" in a special compartment adjoining the main cabin for extra-fast delivery upon arrival.

# What Made Us Laugh

"How's this for a second honeymoon?"

"Now, let's break the news to Mother."

"I have three teenage daughters!"

"Pardon me, but could I interest you in a 36-inch screen?"

"Come in, Marge, but prepare yourself for a horrible shock!"

"Marry me, Cynthia … and help me pay for it."

"Can you rough it for a while? … I need the extension cord for ironing."

# In the News

Headlining the national news in 1954, a group of four Puerto Rican Nationalists attacked the United States House of Representatives. No one was killed, but the guilty were part of a larger conspiracy to overthrow American influence in Puerto Rico. Los Angeles struggled with smog issues. Pollution had become a serious problem in the city as the numbers of automobiles and highways increased. The crisis set off public outcry and a round of grand jury investigations. Senator Joseph McCarthy continued his assault on communism with a confrontation with the United States Army. He accused Pentagon officials of harboring known Communists. A clash between Army attorney Joseph Welch and McCarthy broke McCarthy's untouchable status, shifted the public mood and censured the senator.

Los Angeles citizens endured nine days of throat-burning and eye-stinging smog in October. Some people even wore gas masks to protect themselves. The foul air smothered the city, shutting down schools and businesses for most of the month.

Senator McCarthy of Wisconsin testifies against the United States Army during the Army v. McCarthy hearings in Washington, D.C. He stands before a map that charts Communist activity in the United States.

## 1954 Trivia

**Q.** What well-known immigration station closed in 1954?

A. Ellis Island in New York Harbor. Twelve million immigrants were processed between 1892 and 1954.

© GETTY IMAGES

## U.S. News

Five Congressmen Wounded by Puerto Rican Nationalists

U.S. Army-McCarthy Hearings

Los Angeles Smog Crisis

"Under God" added to Pledge of Allegiance

Brown Versus Board of Education

Black student Nathaniel Steward recites his lesson surrounded by classmates at Saint-Dominique school in Washington, D.C., on May 21, 1954. This is the first time the Brown v. Board of Education decision outlawing segregation in state schools is applied. Some Southern leaders were shaken by the verdict and quickly passed legislation, declaring they would not integrate at all.

Schoolchildren recite a new version of the Pledge of Allegiance that includes the words "under God." The additional words were signed into law on Flag Day, 1954. In a country that was predominantly Christian, the new addition was widely applauded.

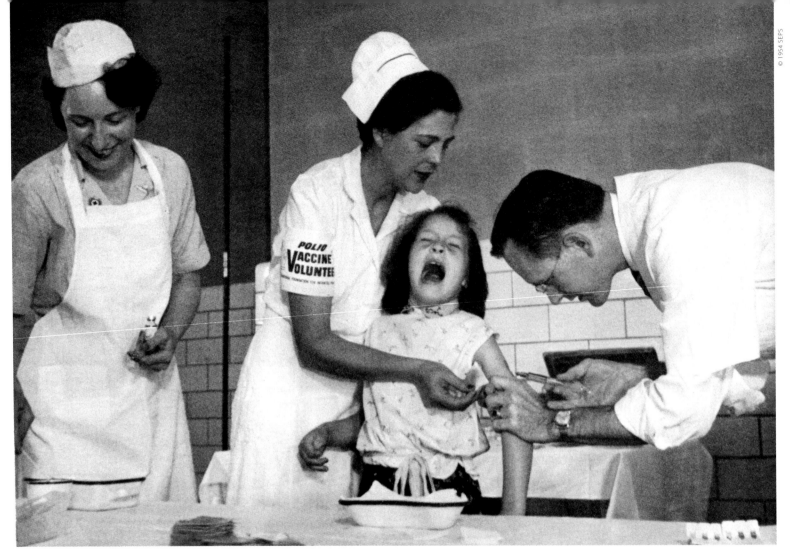

Nurses assist a doctor in giving a Salk polio vaccination.

Anxious second-graders line up for their shots during a mass test of the Salk polio vaccine. More than 1.8 million schoolchildren were injected with the vaccination.

# In the News

## Medical highlights

Polio vaccine field trials were held nationally in 1954. A series of three or four injections was required to make someone immune. Vaccine developer Jonas Salk proved it was safe by testing it on himself, his wife and his children. The first successful organ transplant in humans was performed with identical twins, Ronald and Richard Herrik, by Dr. Joseph Murray at the Peter Bent Brigham Hospital in Boston. Kidneys became the most frequently transplanted organ. In 1954 it became U.S. national policy to subsidize health insurance through tax reforms. The Internal Revenue Service decreed that health insurance premiums paid by employers were exempt from income tax.

Dr. Joseph Murray, upper left, is shown with twins Ronald Herrik, left front, and Richard, right front. Ronald donated a kidney to Richard during a 5½-hour surgery that rejuvenated the whole field of transplantation. Dr. Murray went on to win a Nobel Prize in Medicine in 1990.

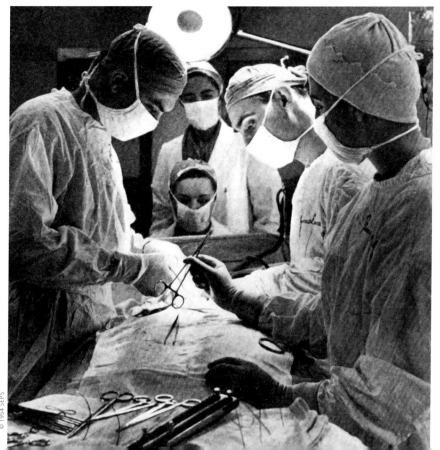

As new hospitals were being built, surgery rooms and equipment became more efficient.

# In the News

## World events

In an effort to broaden its sphere of communist influence, the Soviet Union began a wide-reaching program to distribute foreign aid to noncommunist Third World nations. In other world news, delegates from the U.S., Vietnam, Laos, Cambodia, France, the Soviet Union, China and Great Britain convened at the Geneva Conference on Indochina in an effort to reach consensus on the unrest in Southeast Asia. The Geneva Accords agreed upon at the conference went into effect, dividing Vietnam into North and South at the 17th parallel. In Europe, nine years after the end of World War II, food rationing finally came to an end in Great Britain.

An avalanche in the Alps at Blons, Austria, was one of the worst recorded at that time, killing hundreds of people in only 10 hours.

Vietnamese civilians, mainly peasants, walk bicycles loaded with food and munitions on a road leading to the Dien Bien Phu battlefield. The epic battle precipitated the collapse of French colonial rule in Indochina. The siege was one of the defining events in the history of Southeast Asia.

# World News

### Outstanding Events

Avalanches in Austrian Alps
Kills Hundreds

Siege in Southeast Asia

Nasser Becomes Prime
Minister of Egypt

Vietnam Divided into
North and South

Colonel Gamal Abdel Nasser became the prime minister of
Egypt. In October, Egypt and Great Britain reached a consensus
on terms to end the 72-year British occupation of the Suez Canal.
Seated are Prime Minister Nasser, right, and British Minister of
State Anthony Nutting, left, who are signing the treaty.

Norman Rockwell painted this portrait of comedian Bob Hope with fun in his eyes and a mischievous grin. The painting was featured on the cover of the Feb. 13, 1954, edition of *The Saturday Evening Post*.

Songstress Margaret Whiting and funnyman Phil Harris join Bob in some clowning for the audience after his radio show broadcast from Hollywood.

Bob Hope and Bing Crosby performed together and were close friends. Bing said, "People are always asking me how Hope survives the schedule he sets for himself. He couldn't survive without it. Applause, laughter and commendation are food and drink for him."

The photo above was taken at a rehearsal for Bob Hope's television show.

# Bob Hope, Thanks for the Memories

Bob Hope was born in England on May 29, 1903, and moved with his family to Cleveland, Ohio, in 1907. He became one of the most recognized profiles and talents in the world. Bob's success as a radio comedian led to Hollywood and a contract with Paramount. In the entire history of show business, no individual traveled so far or so often to entertain so many. For nearly six decades, whether our country was at war or at peace, Bob traveled the globe to entertain American servicemen and women. The media dubbed him "America's No. 1 Soldier in Greasepaint." To those serving our country, he was "G.I. Bob" and their clown hero. He was married to his wife, Delores, for 69 years until he died on July 27, 2003.

Dean Cole, left, decorates Bob in matronly style for a film role and his agent, Louis Shurr, right, is amused.

## Bob Hope Trivia

Q. What was the first movie Bob Hope starred in with Bing Crosby?

A. Road to Singapore

"Nora," said Bob of his dancing daughter, "is a natural-born ham." Daughter Linda, wife Dolores and Bob accompany her. Bob's sons, Tony and Kelly, and Aunt Alice are her audience. Bob enjoyed music, and he is known for his theme song, "Thanks for the Memories."

## Tops *at the* Box Office

White Christmas

20,000 Leagues
Under the Sea

Rear Window

Carmen Jones

The Caine Mutiny

The Country Girl

The Barefoot Contessa

A Star Is Born

The High and the Mighty

Magnificent Obsession

The Long, Long Trailer

On the Waterfront

# The Big Screen

*White Christmas* was the top-grossing film of 1954. In the movie, a successful song-and-dance team become romantically involved with a sister act and team up to save the failing Vermont inn of their former commanding general. *On the Waterfront* was about an ex-prizefighter who struggled to stand up to corrupt bosses. Marlon Brando was paid $100,000 for his role in the movie. It produced Oscars for Marlon Brando for Best Actor, Eva Marie Saint for Best Supporting Actress, Elia Kazan for Best Director and the coveted Best Motion Picture award. A Walt Disney Production, *20,000 Leagues Under the Sea*, was a top-quality movie considered to be the best adaptation on film of a science-fiction story by Jules Verne.

Actors James Mason, Kirk Douglas, Peter Lorre and Paul Lukas dine and talk in a luxuriously appointed submarine called the *Nautilus* in a scene from the movie *20,000 Leagues Under the Sea.*

From left, actors Bing Crosby as Bob Wallace, Rosemary Clooney as Betty Haynes, Vera-Ellen as Judy Haynes and Danny Kay as Phil Davis sing together in a scene from the movie *White Christmas*. The musical produced hit songs written by Irving Berlin, including the perennial classic, "White Christmas." The version sung by Bing Crosby became one of the best-selling singles of all time.

**1954 Trivia**

**Q.** Where was *On the Waterfront* filmed?

A. Hoboken, N.J.

*Carmen Jones* featured Harry Belafonte as Joe, Dorothy Dandridge as Carmen and Pearl Bailey as Frankie. The movie won a Golden Globe for Best Motion Picture in the musical/comedy area.

Marlon Brando starred as Terry Malloy and Eva Marie Saint was Edie Doyle in the movie *On the Waterfront*.

# DAILY 📷 NEWS
### NEW YORK'S PICTURE NEWSPAPER®

4¢

Vol. 35. No. 175   Copr. 1954 News Syndicate Co. Inc.   New York 17, N.Y., Friday, January 15, 1954★   4¢ IN CITY LIMITS / 5¢ OUTSIDE CITY LIMITS

# MARILYN WEDS JOE DiMAGGIO

————Story on Page 3

**DiMaggio Signs With a New Manager.** Joe DiMaggio plants a kiss on the luscious Marilyn Monroe just before leaving San Francisco City Hall where they were married yesterday. Simple wedding of former Yankee star and movie actress drew nearly 400 spectators. (Associated Press Wirephoto) —Story on page 3

The marriage of Marilyn Monroe and Joe DiMaggio on Jan. 14, 1954 was front-page news the next day. Later in the year, Monroe took the part of The Girl in the movie *The Seven Year Itch*, in which the famous scene of Monroe standing over a subway exhaust was filmed. Marilyn and Joe argued over the scene later that year, and she filed for divorce in October 1954.

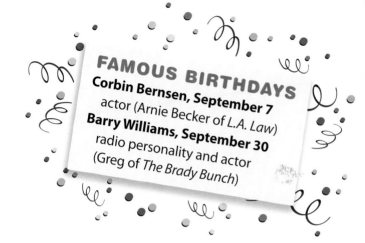

Perennial villain actor Jack Palance, right, visits Frank Sinatra and Doris Day on the set of the movie *Young at Heart*.

Tina Louise, who later portrayed Ginger on the *Gilligan's Island* TV show, dines with Italian opera singer Cesare Siepi.

# Unforgettable Icons

The stars of 1954 were symbols of success, avidly pursued and imitated by their fans. Marilyn Monroe, one of Hollywood's greatest superstars and an all-time sex symbol, married baseball great Joe DiMaggio. Frank Sinatra, American singer and motion-picture actor, was one of the most sought-after performers in the entertainment industry. He was often hailed as the greatest American singer of 20th-century popular music. Doris Day's performances in movie musicals of the 1950s made her a leading Hollywood star. Groucho Marx, comedian, actor, singer and writer, spent decades making people laugh with his snappy one-liners and sharp wit.

Baseball star Stan Musial signs autographs for young St. Louis Cardinals fans. He was nicknamed "Stan the Man" and was widely considered to be one of the greatest hitters in baseball history. He was the idol of thousands of kids and the highest-paid player in National League history in 1954.

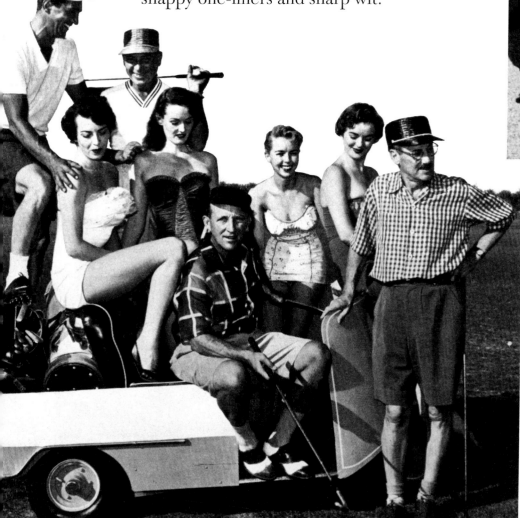

Comedian Groucho Marx, far right, is pictured with Dean Martin, Harpo Marx, Bing Crosby and female fans. He once described his comedy as "the type of humor that made people laugh at themselves." He entertained America with his wisecracks on the TV show *You Bet Your Life*.

# Unforgettable Icons

## Grace Kelly

Grace Kelly was born on Nov. 12, 1929, in Philadelphia, Pa., the third of four children. Her father was a self-made millionaire. She expressed a love of performance at a young age. In addition to participating in school plays and community productions, she occasionally modeled with her mother and sister. After high school, Grace decided to pursue an acting career despite her parents' objections. Gary Cooper discovered Grace Kelly on the set of her first film, *Fourteen Hours* in 1951, when she was 22 years old. He arranged for her to play his very young wife in *High Noon* in 1952, an acclaimed Western movie that put her on the path to stardom. A year later, Kelly was offered a role in *Mogambo*, a film set in Kenya, starring Clark Gable and Ava Gardner. *Mogambo* marked a turning point in Kelly's career; she was nominated for her first Academy Award and won a Golden Globe Award for Best Supporting Actress. In 1954, Kelly was one of the highest-paid and most respected actresses in the world. She married Prince Rainier III of Monaco in 1956, leaving behind the bright lights of Hollywood.

Grace Kelly enjoys a cup of coffee at the MGM commissary with actresses Janet Leigh and Ann Blyth.

"She's a lady, and she expects to be treated like a lady," said Jimmy Stewart of Grace Kelly. "[She's] the thoroughbred type," said Van Johnson.

## 1954 Trivia

**Q.** Who played the role of Grace Kelly's boyfriend in the movie *Rear Window*?

*A. James Stewart*

Actress Grace Kelly in a still from the film *Green Fire*. She was a cool, elegant beauty who also starred in such films as *High Noon* and *To Catch a Thief*.

A soundman holds a mike over Grace, who starred with Stewart Granger in this movie, *Green Fire*. She also played opposite James Stewart, Bing Crosby, William Holden and Cary Grant in other films.

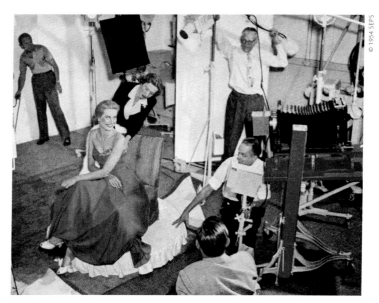

Since her first leading role, Grace was one of the "hottest" properties in Hollywood. Here, in a rare afternoon off from her movie schedule, she poses for publicity shots.

# Unforgettable Icons

## *Famous families*

At his home in North Hollywood, actor William Holden shows his family some 3-D slides he brought back from one of his trips. Holden won an Oscar for Best Actor in a leading role in 1953 for his role as the cynical sergeant in the movie *Stalag 17*.

## Superstars of 1954

Match the first and last names of famous people mentioned in this book.

1. Jackie
2. Joseph
3. Rosemary
4. Mike
5. Grace
6. Maureen

A. Kelly
B. Wallace
C. Gleason
D. Clooney
E. Connolly
F. McCarthy

*Answers: 1-C; 2-F; 3-D; 4-B; 5-A; 6-E.*

An amateur magician, baseball star Stan Musial wows his family with a card trick. After 13 seasons in the majors, Stan still hoped to play "three or four more years."

Left to right, Mrs. Jack Benny, Seth Baker, Mrs. Seth Baker (Joan Benny) and Jack Benny, father of the bride, at Joan's wedding on March 9, 1954.

Comedian Groucho Marx meets his daughter, Melinda, at her Hollywood school. He himself quit grade school when he was 14 and went to work.

Hungarian-born Hollywood producer Joe Pasternak loved gaiety and specialized in film concoctions full of fun, music and beautiful girls. Here he shares a moment of laughter with his youngest son, Peter.

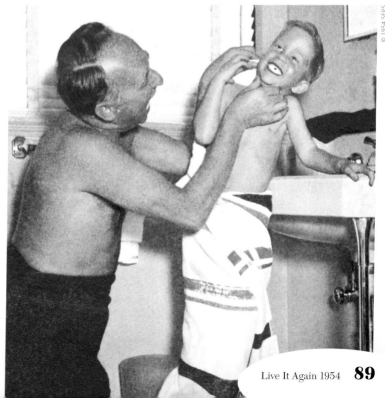

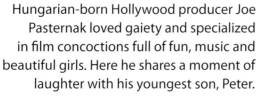

# The Best in Sports

In 1954, Bill Vukovich won the 38th running of the Indianapolis 500 car race. He moved from his 19th-place starting position to first place and a record-shattering 130.840 mph victory. The Minnesota Lakers won the NBA title, victorious four games to three over the Syracuse Nationals. The Montreal Canadiens battled the Detroit Red Wings for the Stanley Cup hockey trophy. Detroit won in game seven in overtime. In tennis, Tony Trabert won the French Open and Mervyn Rose won the Australian Open, while Maureen Connolly, "Little Mo," won the women's singles championship at both the French Open and Wimbledon. Maureen's career was ended by a horseback riding accident right after her Wimbledon victory.

Free-spending horse players gambled more than $2 million at the race tracks, an all-time high. Triple Crown races were won by Determine at the Kentucky Derby, Hasty Road at the Preakness Stakes and High Gun at the Belmont Stakes.

Ted Lindsay of the Detroit Red Wings kisses the cup as manager Jack Adams and the rest of the Wings celebrate winning the Stanley Cup after defeating the Montreal Canadiens in game seven with an overtime score of 2-1.

The 1954 NBA World Champion Minneapolis Lakers pose for a team photo with head coach John Kundla.

American tennis player Maureen Connolly holds the women's singles championship trophy after her victory at Wimbledon.

American tennis player Tony Trabert, left, and Mervyn Rose of Australia walk on to Centre Court before their match at Wimbledon.

Bill Vukovich's car, No. 14, takes the lead at the Indianapolis 500.

Joanne Weaver of the Fort Wayne Daisies was the MVP of the All-American Girls Professional Baseball League. Those who competed not only had to be highly skilled players, they also had to comply with high moral standards and rules of conduct imposed by the League.

The 1954 All-American Girls Professional Baseball League champions were the Kalamazoo Lassies.

World Series winners were the New York Giants. They defeated the Cleveland Indians, who entered the World Series as the favorite after winning 111 regular-season games— an American League record.

# The Best in Sports

## Outstanding athletes

1954 was the last year for the All-American Girls Professional Baseball League, due to the rise of other forms of recreation and entertainment, and televised major league games. The champs were the Kalamazoo Lassies. The New York Giants beat the Cleveland Indians in four games to win baseball's World Series. Willie Mays of the New York Giants made an incredible over-the-shoulder catch in game one of the series. It was one of the most famous catches in World Series history. The Cleveland Browns defeated the Detroit Lions for the NFL championship.

U.S. Open golf champion Ed Furgol practices a trap shot.

Rocky Marciano, right, retained his world heavyweight title by defeating Ezzard Charles, left, in New York City on Sept. 17, 1954. Marciano was remembered for his tough-guy, never-say-die style.

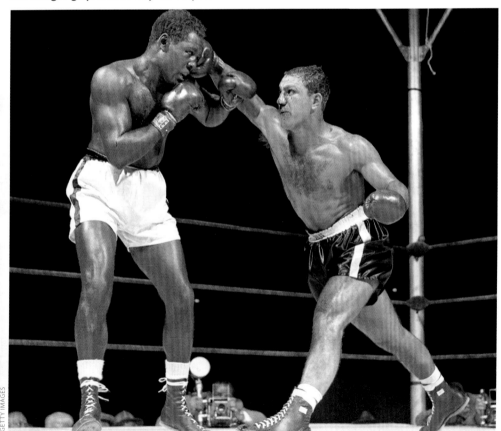

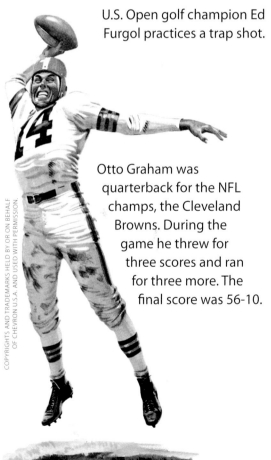

Otto Graham was quarterback for the NFL champs, the Cleveland Browns. During the game he threw for three scores and ran for three more. The final score was 56-10.

# What Made Us Laugh

"Would you mind if Quincey tags along?
He's in love with me too."

"ALL I WANT IS TWO GALLONS OF GAS … ALL I …"

"I'd like a dress that would make me look sophisticated
without making my father blow his top."

"Let's wait and see if they both hang up at the same time."

"Why do I drive you to distraction, Mommy?"

"While you were phoning, I ordered for both of us."

"Now, isn't that just like being at the game?"

"My husband's taking me out for another driving lesson."

# Leading Ladies of *The Post*

*The Saturday Evening Post* featured imaginative illustrations for fictional stories that were regularly included in each edition. The Leading Ladies of *The Post* are a collection of images from these often steamy romance stories. Artists were challenged to interpret these stories on canvas, and we have included a sampling of the Leading Ladies of 1954. The sultry, fashion-forward heroines of the tales are featured along with the original article captions.

He'd bought an island to escape this dizzy dame. But when he moved in, she was parked on his beach.

She looked at him with contempt. She didn't have to say a word. She turned to the gentleman-type and said, "Shall we go, Clarence?"

They expected a dear little lady with snowy hair and a lace cap. And then in walked the fabulous grandma.

She offered to help him win his girl back. And, like a dope, he took her up on it.

She fell for a scientist who had mastered the laws of nature and knew nothing about women. But she had all the answers.

She was so prettily contrite that she was soon forgiven. Just then a nightclub photographer came to the table.

Her body swayed seductively toward him. "You've done so much for me— do this one more thing? Give me my chance?"

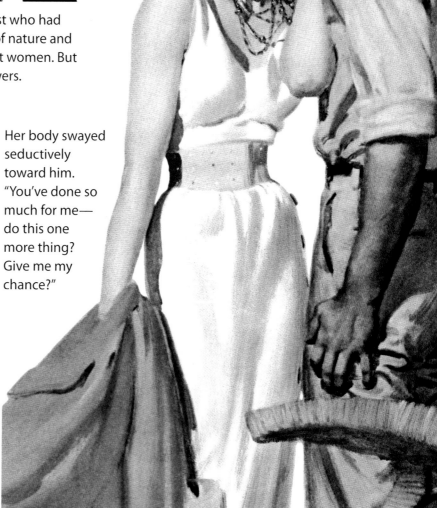

Handmacher was the master tailor to the American woman. The suit above was crisp and cool with a smooth fit and sold for $29.95.

The popular look in sweaters was a soft appearance, styled along simple lines. Prices ranged from $2.98 for individual sweaters to $6.98 for sets.

Eye-catching one-piece swimsuits were a favorite hit in 1954.

"Another new hat, Mrs. Bremer— how do you manage to afford it?"

# Fashionable in 1954

American dollars made the United States the fashion center of the world. American women had money to spend for clothes in 1954, but they were more selective buyers. They had to be satisfied with quality and value as well as fashion before loosening purse strings. They demanded diversified clothes for multiple activities. Women wanted casual clothes in which they could feel young and live comfortably. Skirts were conservative and below the knee, and there were an equal number of full and straight ones.

1954 MONTGOMERY WARD

Fashion-conscious women chose matching hats, gloves and purses.

The red dress was casual with a full skirt and sold for $12.98. The blue dress was 100 percent wool with a slim, pleated skirt and cost $16.98.

New lightweight nylon was used for cool, soft nightwear.

**The Metro Daily News**

THE WEATHER

FINAL EDITION

FIVE CENTS

SEPTEMBER 11, 1954

## MISS AMERICA PAGEANT BROADCAST ON TELEVISION FOR THE FIRST TIME.

Lee Meriwether (Calif.) was crowned for her future role as Miss America 1955.

Handsome, foot-cooling shoes by Roblee ranged in price from $9.95 to $15.95.

# Fashionable in 1954

## Dressed for Success

Clothes made the man of 1954. Single-breasted men's flannel suits were worn at the office. Casual wear was cool, comfortable and colorful. Button-up shirts were fleecy soft, washable and available in checks, plaids and solid colors with neat, comfortable collars. Men took summer in stride with mesh shoes. They were "air-conditioned" combinations of patterned nylon mesh and lightweight leather, the smartest and surest way to keep cool.

© 1954 SEPS

"From back here it looks quite jaunty."

Smart nylon dress socks came in assorted designs and cost $1.34 for two pairs.

1954 MONTGOMERY WARD

1954 MONTGOMERY WARD

Distinctive argyle socks in a four-diamond pattern were priced at $1.19 a pair.

Arrow shirts sold for about $8 each.

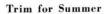

Wembley ties were available in fine, French-imported satins, paneled basket weaves and fashionable woven argyle designs.

Accessories by Buxton reflected style with matching key holders and billfolds.

## Trim for Summer

During the dog days, a man's next-best friend is very likely to be his Dixie Weave Bengaline tropical by Hart Schaffner & Marx. More than a mere summer-weight, the Bengaline tropical worsted is ingeniously "ventilated" by as many as 14,600,000 tiny pores! And by reversing the twist in certain threads even more "breathing spaces" are created. Wonderfully cooperative about shedding wrinkles, too. Why not see what wonders a Dixie Weave Bengaline can do for *your* summer spirits? For the address of the dealer most convenient to you, write Hart Schaffner & Marx, Dept. P5, 36 S. Franklin St., Chicago 6, Ill.

DIXIE WEAVE—Reg. U. S. Pat. Off.

*One of the newest DIXIE WEAVE BENGALINE colors is the cool and modern summer charcoal, shown here in the tall, trim Trend model.*

## HART SCHAFFNER & MARX

### The Metro Daily News

THE WEATHER
City and State—Rain,
turning to Fair today

FINAL EDITION

VOLUME 65 — No. 181

35 PAGES          FIVE CENTS

**OCTOBER 1, 1954**

# AUTOMOBILE MANUFACTURERS STUDEBAKER AND PACKARD MERGE TO FORM THE STUDEBAKER-PACKARD CORP.

Matching sister dresses ranged in price from $2.98 to $5.98 each.

Boys' coat sweaters were priced at $2.98.

Girls' outerwear was available in a wide variety of styles and was priced from $11.98 to $19.98 per set.

Colorful plaid boys' shirts sold for $1.98 and Lone Ranger sweatshirts cost $1.29.

# Fashionable in 1954

## Children's wear

"My-sister-and-me" fashions were popular. Dainty dresses with full-circle skirts and plaid school dresses flattered look-alike sisters with colorful hues. Coats were water-repellent or made of wool with matching slacks, complete with adjustable suspenders. Popular playwear for tiny tots was the one-piece, with snaps for easy changing. Some had attached feet for extra warmth and protection.

What type of clothes did you wish for when you were a child?

Buckin' Bronco waterproof over-the-shoes boots had non-skid rubber soles and sold for about $3.30.

One-piece creeperalls for toddlers were priced from $1.98 to $3.98.

Little puddle jumpers yearned for rainy days with Donald Duck for a playmate. These rubber boots sold for $1.45.

Evelyn Ay, representative of the state of Pennsylvania, experienced a dream coming true when she became Miss America 1954.

# When I Grow Up ...

Just like now, little boys and girls dreamed big dreams for the future and could hardly wait to grow up, especially when they had older siblings. The grown-up life seemed so glamorous to the very young. Girls wondered if they would grow up to be Miss America and practiced the perfect winner's wave and elegant walk. Boys looked up to sports heroes and pilots. Teenagers made plans to go to college to reach their goals.

**FAMOUS BIRTHDAYS**
**Dennis Eckersley, October 3** baseball pitcher (St. Louis Cardinals)
**Robert A. Schuller, October 7** televangelist and author

She's growing up. Yesterday she mothered her doll, and today she wants to look 15 years older.

NORMAN ROCKWELL

Baseball hero "Stan the Man" Musial signs autographs for eager fans.

Father's loneliness will soon change into the satisfaction of watching his lad making a go of things in the grown-up world.

Downstairs a man waits, while a little sister watches her older sister's magic with amazement. She doubts that boys are worth so much work—a doubt she'll soon get over.

Pilots are heroes and role models, especially just after landing in low visibility. As the procedure is explained, the little boy listens with wide-eyed wonder.

School opened young eyes to the wonders of the big world outside their neighborhoods.

Remember the Dick and Jane reading series? The books relied on repetition, using phrases like, "Oh, see. Oh, see Jane. Funny, funny Jane."

Children developed their artistic skills with paints in all the colors of the rainbow.

The Metro Daily News

FINAL EDITION

NOVEMBER 2, 1954

**STROM THURMOND OF SOUTH CAROLINA BECOMES THE FIRST SENATOR ELECTED BY A WRITE-IN VOTE**

Sen. Thurmond held this office for 48 years, retiring at the age of 100.

# School Days

For the uninitiated, the first day of school sometimes created butterflies in the stomach. Children were fortunate when the bus driver was caring and friendly. From riding the bus and eating in the cafeteria, to doing homework and going to assemblies, school marked the first time children ventured off to chart their own course. Yes, school days were always an adventure. Beyond the books was recess, that most-anticipated part of the school day. Children had morning, noon and afternoon recess and played Red Rover and baseball, and climbed trees and the monkey bars.

That first school dance was a big event. Of course, you wanted to look your best, so the decision about what to wear was mighty important.

School is dismissed for the day and the race for home and the craving for milk and cookies begins.

"Mississippi. M—eeeek—I—eeeek—
S—eeeek—S—eeeek—I—eeeek—
S—eeeek—S—eeeek—"

During the halftime at high school football games, bands marched behind girls who twirled batons.

# School Days

## The teen years

Most of us have very clear memories of our high school days. We used typewriters and were able to go home for lunch or stay at school and eat in the cafeteria. There were bells to signal the beginning and end of classes and an occasional fire drill. The typical desk was a table connected to the chair with a basket underneath meant for holding books, and classes ranged from home economics to algebra. The majority of teenagers did their best to dress like everyone else, to have dates for football games and dances, and to cruise around town with a carload of friends. The aim was to seem normal and never to be called "square."

Teenage girls spent hours perfecting their hair and makeup in hopes of attracting attention at the school dance.

After classes many teens walked home and shared the important events of the day.

Some girls sewed their own clothes, after learning sewing techniques in home economics class.

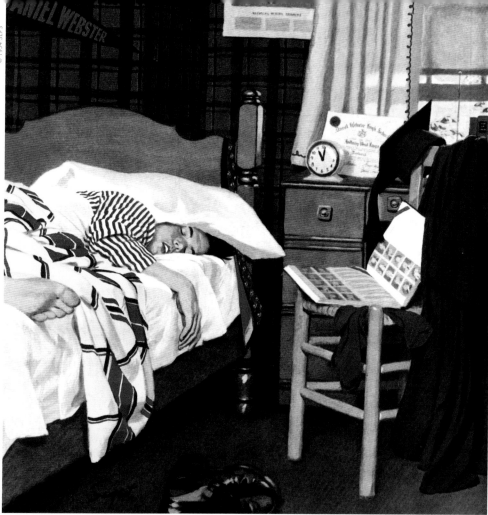

Sleeping in is a luxury after a full schedule of senior-year activities. Perhaps this boy is dreaming about his girl, the prettiest in the high school yearbook.

Driver's education began with classroom learning and progressed to time behind the wheel.

"Hello, Mrs. Williams? This is Sue—I was wondering if I can expect any sitting jobs from you this month?"

Girl Scouts brought girls of all backgrounds into the outdoors, giving them the opportunity to learn about nature, and to develop self-reliance and resourcefulness.

Students started their FFA experience by joining a local chapter at their school, where the agriculture teacher served as chapter advisor. Members received recognition through competition and award programs.

Cub Scouts, the youngest group of Boy Scouts, race cars at an event. The Boy Scout motto is still, "Be prepared."

# The Clubs We Joined

After-school club-membership numbers grew as children took part in FFA, 4-H, Boy Scouts and Girl Scouts. FFA was the abbreviation for Future Farmers of America, a club that brought together students, teachers and agribusiness to encourage agricultural education. As one of the first youth-development organizations in America, 4-H came from the desire to make public school education more connected to country life. Boy Scouts and Girl Scouts had goals to train youth in responsible citizenship, character development and self-reliance through participation in a wide range of outdoor activities and educational programs. Children enjoyed meeting and working with others for a common goal.

At older age levels, Boy Scouts worked in partnership with community organizations.

Members of 4-H often raised and showed animals at the county fair, hoping to receive a ribbon for their efforts.

## FFA Trivia

**Q.** When was the FFA organization founded?

A. 1928

Did you value Sunday afternoon naps or stamp collecting with Grandpa?

## Best-Selling Books of 1954

*Not as a Stranger*
by Morton Thompson

*Mary Anne*
by Daphne du Maurier

*Love Is Eternal*
by Irving Stone

*The Royal Box*
by Frances Parkinson Keyes

*The Egyptian*
by Mika Waltari

*No Time for Sergeants*
by Mac Hyman

*Sweet Thursday*
by John Steinbeck

*The View from Pompey's Head*
by Hamilton Basso

*Never Victorious, Never Defeated*
by Taylor Caldwell

*Benton's Row* by Frank Yerby

# Leisure Activities

There's nothing wrong with doing things for pleasure on occasion, and everyone can profit from setting aside time to relax. A hobby is a pleasant change from work and provides a sense of accomplishment while being enjoyable. Doing something for the sheer joy of it is good for the soul. The activity really doesn't matter as the objective is to simply enjoy life in whatever way you prefer.

Free-time activities vary greatly. Some people enjoy socializing, while others like to take walks or work in the garden.

Slumber party? Gee, that's dandy!
Look your sharpest, everyone!
Snappy PJ's come in handy —
"Fresh up" parties sure are fun!

**FAMOUS BIRTHDAYS**
**Condoleezza Rice, November 14**
former United States Secretary of State
**Kathleen Quinlan, November 19**
actress

Copyright 1954 by The Seven-Up Company

# "Fresh up" with Seven-Up!

**THE ALL-FAMILY DRINK!** Enjoy sparkling, crystal-clear 7-Up . . . often. Seven-Up is so pure, so good, so wholesome that everybody — from tiny tots to grandmas and all ages in between — may "fresh up" to his heart's content. And 7-Up makes *food* taste *extra* good. So have a Stackwich with chilled 7-Up. Buy 7-Up wherever you see those bright 7-Up signs. **You like it ... it likes you!**

**Get a family supply** of 24 bottles. Buy 7-Up by the case. Or get the handy **7-Up Family Pack.** Easy-lift center handle, easy to store.

FAMILY PACK

7up
REG. U.S. PAT. OFF.

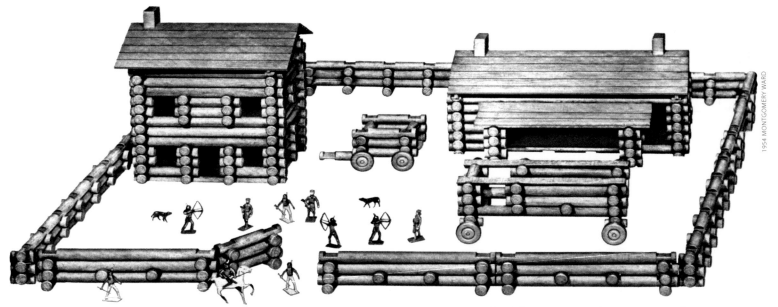

Lincoln Logs were used to build pioneer settlements complete with cabins, ranch houses, bunk houses and wagons. No glue was needed, and they could be reused for countless projects.

"Call Me Lucky," Bing Crosby's board game, sold for $2.72.

Scrabble was a word game that really took off in 1954. The lettered tile game was a favorite for parents because of the focus on vocabulary and word building.

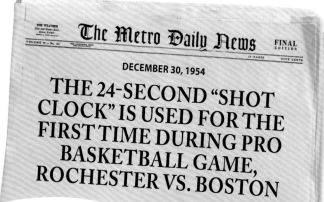

The Metro Daily News

FINAL EDITION

DECEMBER 30, 1954

THE 24-SECOND "SHOT CLOCK" IS USED FOR THE FIRST TIME DURING PRO BASKETBALL GAME, ROCHESTER VS. BOSTON

# Child's Play

Toys are honest-to-goodness fun. They tell the story of our childhood and hold memories of those growing-up years. Model trains were a favorite toy of boys in 1954. It was during the 1950s that an emphasis on realism in model trains began to catch on. There were exciting extras available such as real smoke and remote-controlled whistles. Scrabble, the classic word game, became popular with sales of around 4 million. Lincoln Logs were a simple, durable wooden construction toy with endless creative possibilities.

Model fighter planes came in kits with instructions, pieces, glue and decals. This five-plane set sold for $1.98.

Kids could use potatoes, fruit or clay to create funny faces with a Mr. and Mrs. Potato Head kit. It sold for $1.69.

Fathers could start a new comradeship with sons by sharing the matchless thrills of railroading and the satisfaction of building bigger and better sets. A Lionel Train set could be bought for about $20.

Give little girls a coloring book and a set of crayons, and most will be happily engrossed for hours.

# Child's Play
## Especially for girls

Girls treasured their dolls and many hours were filled with dressing, feeding, bathing and rocking them. Many dolls had "rooted" hair, perfect for children who liked to comb, wave and arrange their doll's hair. Dainty miniature dolls were also popular. They were made of plastic with movable heads and arms, and sleeping eyes. Little girls enjoyed the make-believe world of talking on the telephone and playing nurse, pretending to be a grown-up with dress-up clothes and accessories.

This deluxe plastic nurse kit included a stethoscope, microscope, pretend pills and dress-up outfit, and sold for $3.69.

Lovable dolls had washable latex bodies that felt like real baby skin. They were available in sizes that ranged from 14 to 26 inches tall and cost from $4.75 to $11.75.

Toy telephones inspired long conversations with imaginary friends.

Tiny dolls, including miniature brides and grooms, had painted shoes and mohair wigs, and sold for about $1.50 each.

This three-speed phonograph came with 12 children's records and a record rack for $34.50.

Buying, wrapping, giving and receiving gifts enhance the spirit of the holiday season.

"Santa, bend down so I can whisper in your ear. I'd like you to know about a special toy I've been hoping will be under the Christmas tree," requests the child, anticipating Christmas morning.

© 1954 SEPS

Nancy Wolterworth

© 1954 SEPS

# Yuletide Memories

In the Dec. 18, 1954 edition of *The Post*, the American Cyanamid Co. placed an ad with the photo at right along with this fitting copy: "Because of Christmas, all of us capture some of the wonder and joy and faith that shine in children's eyes. Because of Christmas, we feel again the happiness that comes with gift-giving. Because of Christmas, we shall be a little more patient, and more tolerant and understanding; we shall draw a little closer to our families, our friends and our neighbors. Because of the magic of Christmas Day, we shall think a little more deeply about the teachings that have survived through the centuries to preserve for us the greatest message of hope and good will the world has ever known."

CHRISTMAS GREETINGS
FROM
THE CUNNINGHAMS

FAMOUS BIRTHDAYS

**Stone Phillips, December 2**
journalist

**Denzel Washington, December 28**
actor

Christmas cards are one of the heartwarming aspects of the yuletide season, especially when family photos are included.

The Saturday Evening

# POST

January 9, 1954 — 15¢

An Ex-Government Worker Overseas Says
**I RODE UNCLE SAM'S GRAVY TRAIN**

**THEY DON'T TELL THE TRUTH
ABOUT THE SOUTH!**
By Herbert Ravenel Sass

# More *The Saturday Evening Post* Covers

*The Saturday Evening Post* covers were works of art, many illustrated by famous artists of the time, including Norman Rockwell. Most of the 1954 covers have been incorporated within the previous pages of this book; the few that were not are presented on the following pages for your enjoyment.

The Saturday Evening

# POST

January 16, 1954 — 15¢

The Man the Reds Couldn't Conquer:
**THE ORDEAL OF
CHAPLAIN KAPAUN**

That Southern Inferiority Complex!
By BERNARD DeVOTO

I wish to see—the Discovery of a Plan, that would in-duce & oblige Nations to settle their Disputes without first Cutting one another's Throats.—When will Men be convinc'd, that even suc-cessful Wars at length be-come Misfortunes to those who unjustly commenc'd them, & who triumph'd blindly in their Success, not seeing all its Consequences.

Benj Franklin 1780

The Saturday Evening

# POST

January 23, 1954 — 15¢

At Last . . .
**GENERAL DEAN**
Tells the Story of His
**CAPTURE, TORTURE
and IMPRISONMENT**

The Saturday Evening
**POST**
January 30, 1954 - 15¢

GENERAL DEAN TELLS HOW
HE WAS "BRAIN-WASHED"

An Intimate Look at
EISENHOWER'S WORKING DAY

The Saturday Evening
**POST**
March 20, 1954 - 15¢

New York's Communist Cop
By CRAIG THOMPSON

THIS IS ON ME
By Bob Hope

The Saturday Evening
**POST**
March 27, 1954 - 15¢

MANHATTAN'S
TEEN-AGE
CRIMINALS
ARE MY JOB

By Marjorie Rittwagen, M.D.

The Saturday Evening
**POST**
April 17, 1954 - 15¢

THAT REMINDS ME—
Former Vice-President
Alben W. Barkley
Tells His Own Story

The Saturday Evening
**POST**
May 8, 1954 - 15¢

DON'T TELL ME
TEACHING'S A SOFT JOB!
By a Public Schoolteacher

HARVEY KUENN:
Baseball's $55,000 Bargain

The Saturday Evening
POST
May 15, 1954 – 15¢

HOW I ESCAPED THE RED TRAP
By JOHN HVASTA,
American Victim
of a Communist Frame-Up

ACQUARIUM
ADMISSION 25¢
CHILDREN FREE

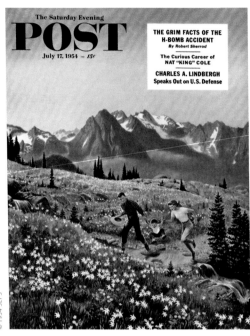

The Saturday Evening
POST
July 17, 1954 – 15¢

THE GRIM FACTS OF THE
H-BOMB ACCIDENT
By Robert Sherrod

The Curious Career of
NAT "KING" COLE

CHARLES A. LINDBERGH
Speaks Out on U.S. Defense

© 1954 SEPS

The Saturday Evening
POST
July 24, 1954 – 15¢

Chief Justice Earl Warren's
Greatest Moment
By BEVERLY SMITH

The Case That Has Shocked Europe:
THE QUEEN OF MURDERS

© 1954 SEPS

© 1954 SEPS

The Saturday Evening
POST
July 31, 1954 – 15¢

Available for Adoption:
BABIES FOR THE BRAVE

HOW I LEARNED TO WIN
IN THE MAJORS
By Carl Erskine, of the Dodgers

WILL NEW ORLEANS
LOSE ITS RIVER?

The Saturday Evening
POST
August 14, 1954 – 15¢

THE TRUTH ABOUT
FLORIDA'S RED TIDE
By Henry La Cossitt

Baseball's Prize Castoff
By William Barry Furlong

JOHN FALTER

© 1954 SEPS

The Saturday Evening
POST
September 4, 1954 – 15¢

FDR, Jr. —
Can He Get His Father's
Old Job?

ED FURGOL,
Golf's Amazing Champ,
Tells His Own Story

© 1954 SEPS

The Saturday Evening
# POST
November 6, 1954 - 15¢

**That Sassy Young Coach
at Iowa**

**"SHOT BY ACCIDENT—"
THEY DIDN'T MEAN TO KILL**
By Ashley Halsey, Jr.

The Saturday Evening
# POST
December 25, 1954 - 15¢

**Bert LaBrucherie,
Former Head Coach at UCLA,
Tells Why
BIG-TIME FOOTBALL
IS NOT FOR HIM!**

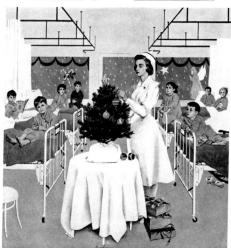

The Saturday Evening
# POST
September 18, 1954 - 15¢

**ARTHUR MARX TELLS THE TRUE STORY
OF HIS AMAZING FATHER:
MY
OLD MAN
GROUCHO**

The Saturday Evening
# POST
October 16, 1954 - 15¢

**An Ivy League Star Says:
I'LL TAKE
HARVARD FOOTBALL!**

**TV's SHRIEKING GENIUS**
By Sidney Shalett

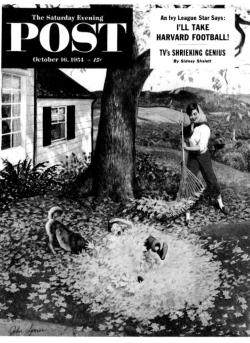

The Saturday Evening
# POST
December 4, 1954 - 15¢

**IN THIS ISSUE**
• Wilderness Cure for Juvenile Delinquency
• Hypothermia—Startling Surgical Technique
• Those Mysterious "Sonic Boom" Explosions
• The Best-Mannered Children in the World

The Saturday Evening
# POST
December 18, 1954 - 15¢

**A Report on Labor's
Coming Battle
For the Guaranteed Annual Wage
ME AND BENNY GOODMAN**
By Lionel Hampton

© 1954 SEPS

**MORE FAMOUS BIRTHDAYS**

**January 5**
**Alex English,** basketball player

**January 6**
**Anthony Minghella,** film director

**January 12**
**Howard Stern,** "Radio's Bad Boy"

**January 14**
**Jim Duggan,** wrestler

**January 17**
**Robert F. Kennedy, Jr.,** attorney

**January 19**
**Steve DeBerg,** NFL quarterback
**Cindy Sherman,** photographer

**January 27**
**Peter Laird,** comic-book artist

**January 28**
**Rick Warren,** pastor and author

**February 1**
**Billy Mumy,** actor (Will Robinson of
    *Lost in Space*)

**February 5**
**Cliff Martinez,** composer

**February 10**
**Larry McWilliams,** baseball pitcher

**February 15**
**Matt Groening,** cartoonist (*The Simpsons*)

**February 17**
**Rene Russo,** actress

**February 20**
**Anthony Stewart Head,** actor
**Patty Hearst,** kidnap victim

**February 28**
**Brian Billick,** football coach

**March 4**
**Peter Erling Jacobsen,** PGA golfer
**Adrian Zmed,** actor

**March 5**
**Marsha Warfield,** comedian and actress

**March 15**
**Craig Wasson,** actor

**March 16**
**Hollis Stacy,** LPGA golfer

**March 17**
**Lesley-Anne Down,** actress

**March 23**
**Geno Auriemma,** basketball coach

**March 24**
**Donna Pescow,** actress
**Robert Carradine,** actor

**April 5**
**Christopher S. Nelson,** actor

**April 7**
**Donna White,** LPGA golfer
**Tony Dorsett,** NFL running back (Dallas
    Cowboys)

**April 9**
**Dennis Quaid,** actor

**April 10**
**Peter MacNicol,** actor (John Cage of
    *Ally McBeal*)

**April 14**
**Bruce Sterling,** author

**April 16**
**Ellen Barkin,** actress

**April 21**
**James Morrison,** actor

**April 23**
**Michael Moore,** film director

**April 29**
**Jerry Seinfeld,** comedian

**May 5**
**John Greg Adams,** PGA golfer
**Dave Spector,** actor

**May 7**
**Amy Heckerling,** film director

**May 8**
**David Keith,** actor (*Firestarter*)
**Pat Meyers,** LPGA golfer

**May 20**
**James Henderson,** country singer
    (Black Oak Arkansas)

**May 21**
**Marc Ribot,** musician

**May 23**
**Marvin Hagler,** boxer

**June 1**
**Jeffrey S. Ashby,** astronaut

**June 2**
**Dennis Haysbert,** actor (President David
    Palmer of *24*)

**June 9**
**George Pérez,** comic-book artist

**June 11**
**Gary Fencik,** NFL defensive back (Chicago Bears)

**June 13**
**Jorge Santana,** guitarist

**June 14**
**Will Patton,** actor (*Remember the Titans*)

**June 19**
**Kathleen Turner,** actress

**June 22**
**Freddie Prinze,** comedian and actor (*Chico and
    The Man*)

**June 28**
**Ava Barber,** country singer (*Lawrence
    Welk Show*)

June 29
**Rick Honeycutt,** baseball pitcher (Oakland A's, St. Louis Cardinals)

July 4
**Jim Beattie,** baseball pitcher (NY Yankees, Seattle Mariners)

July 5
**Jimmy Crespo,** guitarist (Aerosmith)

July 9
**Debbie Sledge,** vocalist (Sister Sledge)

July 11
**Butch Reed,** professional wrestler

July 13
**Rick Chartraw,** ice hockey player
**Louise Mandrell,** country musician (The Mandrell Sisters)

July 18
**Ricky Skaggs,** country musician

July 28
**Bruce Abbott,** actor

August 2
**Lisa Brown,** actress (*Guiding Light* and *As the World Turns*)

August 4
**Janet Coles,** LPGA golfer

August 6
**Paul Steigerwald,** sports announcer

August 12
**Pat Methany,** jazz guitarist

August 16
**James Cameron,** film director

August 20
**William Quinn Buckner,** basketball player
**Don Stark,** actor

August 27
**Derek Warwick,** race car driver

August 29
**Julio Fernandez,** jazz guitarist

September 7
**Michael Emerson,** actor

September 12
**Peter Scolari,** actor (*Bosom Buddies*)

September 18
**Tommy Tuberville,** football coach

September 22
**Shari Belafonte,** actress
**Randy Lanier,** race-car driver

September 25
**Sylvester Croom,** college football coach

September 28
**Steve Largent,** NFL wide receiver (Seattle Seahawks)

October 2
**Lani O'Grady,** actress (Mary of *Eight is Enough*)

October 5
**Wayne Watson,** Christian musician

October 7
**Kenneth Atchley,** composer

October 9
**John O'Hurley,** actor and game-show host
**Scott Bakula,** actor (Dr. Sam Beckett of *Quantum Leap*)

October 13
**George Frazier,** baseball pitcher (Minnesota Twins)

October 19
**Joe Bryant,** basketball player

October 24
**Doug Davidson,** actor (Paul Williams of *The Young & the Restless*)

October 26
**Lauren Tewes,** actress (Julie McCoy of *The Love Boat*)

November 3
**Kevin P. Chilton,** USAF general, astronaut

November 8
**Rickie Lee Jones,** musician

November 11
**Mary Gaitskill,** writer

November 13
**Chris Noth,** actor (Mr. Big of *Sex and the City*)

November 14
**Yanni,** New Age musician

November 16
**Andrea Barrett,** author

November 20
**Frank Marino,** rocker

November 23
**Bruce Hornsby,** musician

November 26
**Roz Chast,** cartoonist

December 11
**Jermaine Jackson,** musician (The Jackson Five)

December 13
**John Anderson,** country musician

December 15
**Alex Cox,** film director
**Justin Ross,** actor

December 19
**Mike Sherman,** college and pro football coach

December 20
**Michael Badalucco,** actor (Jimmy Berluti of *The Practice*)

December 21
**Chris Evert,** tennis player

December 26
**Ozzie Smith,** shortstop (San Diego Padres, St. Louis Cardinals)
**Susan H. Butcher,** dogsled driver

# Facts and Figures of 1954

**President of the U.S.**
Dwight D. Eisenhower
**Vice President of the U.S.**
Richard M. Nixon

**Population of the U.S.**
163,026,000

**Births**
4,017,362

**High School Graduates**
Males: 613,000
Females: 664,000

**Average salary for full-time employee:** $3,967
**Minimum wage (per hour):** $0.75
**Unemployment rate:** 5.5%
**Rate of inflation:** 0.32%

© 1954 SEPS

© GETTY IMAGES

## Average cost for:

Bread (lb.) ............................ $0.17

Bacon (lb.) ............................ $0.82

Butter (lb.) ........................... $0.72

Eggs (doz.) ........................... $0.59

Milk (½ gal.) ......................... $0.46

Potatoes (10 lbs.) ................ $0.53

Coffee (lb.) ........................... $1.11

Sugar (5 lbs.) ....................... $0.53

Gasoline (gal.) ...................... $0.22

Movie ticket ........................ $0.45

Postage stamp .................... $0.03

New home ....................... $10,250

1954 AMERICAN CYANAMID CO.

## Notable Inventions and Firsts

**January 21:** First Lady Mamie Eisenhower christens the first nuclear submarine, the USS *Nautilus*.

**March 1:** Dave Edgerton and James McLamore open the first Burger King restaurant in Miami, Fla., selling burgers and shakes for 18 cents each.

**March 25:** RCA begins mass production of its new color television set. The 12-inch model sells for $1,000.

**April 25:** In a press conference in front of company headquarters, Bell Lab scientists unveil their new invention: the solar cell. The device converts the energy of light directly into electricity.

**June 14:** The United States conducts its first nationally coordinated nuclear attack preparedness drill in cities across the country.

**July 15:** Boeing introduces the 707 passenger jet with a 90-minute maiden flight from Renton Field, located south of Seattle, Wash.

## Sports Winners

**NFL:** Cleveland Browns defeat Detroit Lions
**World Series:** New York Giants defeat Cleveland Indians
**Stanley Cup:** Detroit Red Wings defeat Montreal Canadiens
**The Masters:** Sam Snead
**PGA Championship:** Chick Harbert
**NBA:** Minnesota Lakers defeat Syracuse Nationals.

**September 26:** Actor Ronald Reagan becomes the host of the TV program *General Electric Theater*.

**September 30:** Actress Julie Andrews makes her American debut on Broadway as Polly in the hit show *The Boy Friend*. A critic calls her performance "the season's dramatic highlight."

**October 2:** The World Series is broadcast in color for the first time.

**1954:** Carnation introduced Instant Nonfat Dry Milk. This product was an immediate hit due to its fresh milk flavor when mixed with ice-cold water.

## 1954 Quiz Answers

1. *Dragnet*, page 15
2. Chevrolet's Corvette, page 25
3. *White Christmas*, page 82
4. Tommy Rettig, page 10
5. Greyhound, page 68
6. *I Love Lucy*, page 9
7. Rosemary Clooney, page 6
8. Audrey Hepburn married Mel Ferrer, page 46

# Live It Again 1954

| | |
|---|---|
| PROJECT EDITOR | Barb Sprunger |
| CREATIVE DIRECTOR | Brad Snow |
| COPYWRITER & RESEARCH ASSISTANT | Becky Sarasin |
| COPY SUPERVISOR | Deborah Morgan |
| PRODUCTION ARTIST SUPERVISOR | Erin Brandt |
| PRODUCTION ARTIST | Edith Teegarden |
| COPY EDITOR | Mary O'Donnell, Sam Schneider |
| PHOTOGRAPHY SUPERVISOR | Tammy Christian |
| NOSTALGIA EDITOR | Ken Tate |
| EDITORIAL DIRECTOR | Jeanne Stauffer |
| PUBLISHING SERVICES DIRECTOR | Brenda Gallmeyer |

Printed in China
First Printing: 2011
Library of Congress Control Number: 2011931314

**Customer Service**
LiveItAgain.com
(800) 829-5865

Every effort has been made to ensure the accuracy of the material in this book. However, the publisher is not responsible for research errors or typographical mistakes in this publication.

We would like to thank Curtis Publishing for the art prints used in this book. For fine-art prints and more information on the artists featured in *Live It Again 1954* contact Curtis Publishing, Indianapolis, IN 46202, (317) 633-2070, All rights reserved, www.curtispublishing.com

Works by Norman Rockwell Copyright © 2011 The Norman Rockwell Family Entities.

We would like to thank the Wisconsin Historical Society for the use of their online Photograph and Image collection (www.wisconsinhistory.org) and CNH America LLC.

1 2 3 4 5 6 7 8 9